A Concise and Friendly Guide to Music History

2ND EDITION

Sheryl K. Murphy-Manley, Ph.D.

CENGAGE
Learning™

Australia • Brazil • Japan • Korea • Mexico • Singapore • Spain • United Kingdom • United States

CENGAGE
Learning™

A Concise and Friendly Guide to Music History, 2nd Edition

Sheryl K. Murphy-Manley, Ph.D.

Executive Editors:
Michele Baird

Maureen Staudt

Michael Stranz

Project Development Manager:
Linda deStefano

Senior Marketing Coordinators:
Sara Mercurio

Lindsay Shapiro

Production/Manufacturing Manager:
Donna M. Brown

PreMedia Services Supervisor:
Rebecca A. Walker

Rights & Permissions Specialist:
Kalina Hintz

Cover Image:
Getty Images*

* Unless otherwise noted, all cover images used by Custom Solutions, a part of Cengage Learning, have been supplied courtesy of Getty Images with the exception of the Earthview cover image, which has been supplied by the National Aeronautics and Space Administration (NASA).

For product information and technology assistance, contact us at
Cengage Learning Customer & Sales Support, 1-800-354-9706

For permission to use material from this text or product, submit all requests online at **cengage.com/permissions**
Further permissions questions can be emailed to
permissionrequest@cengage.com

ISBN-13: 978-0-7593-8927-4

ISBN-10: 0-7593-8927-6

Cengage Learning
5191 Natorp Boulevard
Mason, Ohio 45040
USA

Cengage Learning is a leading provider of customized learning solutions with office locations around the globe, including Singapore, the United Kingdom, Australia, Mexico, Brazil, and Japan. Locate your local office at:
international.cengage.com/region

Cengage Learning products are represented in Canada by Nelson Education, Ltd.

For your lifelong learning solutions, visit **custom.cengage.com**

Visit our corporate website at **cengage.com**

Printed in the United States of America

A Concise and Friendly Guide to Music History

❦

An Overview of
Important Composers, Styles, Genres, Forms, Music
Literature and Bibliographic References

Compiled by Sheryl K. Murphy-Manley, Ph.D.

Contents

Preface

The purpose of this compact guide is to help musicians assimilate and summarize the main points concerning music history. This booklet is for the busy musician who would find it useful to have a list of central composers, stylistic traits, popular forms, genres, and instruments from each period.

The guide also presents some of the most famous music literature, both by traditional title and by the more popular title when relevant. For quick reference, the list of compositions is presented in two formats, by composer and by title. Additionally, Chapter 5 and Chapter 6 offer a quick overview of some of the most studied topics concerning world music and jazz history.

This guide is intended to serve several functions:

1. As a review for musicians wishing to prepare for graduate work, including the preparation of entrance and exit exams for colleges and universities
2. As a quick reference guide for music educators and performers
3. As a supplement and study guide for the college music student, and
4. As an introduction to music history for the pre-college level music student

Because this book is a guide, it is by no means a comprehensive representation of the history of music. Rather, this work is meant to serve as a quick and easy reference for the many facts and facets concerning music history and its composers and literature. The contents are directed toward those individuals who already have a working knowledge of the basic elements of music. The fundamentals of musical elements and the reading of music will not be addressed here. (The author assumes that the reader already knows basic terminology of music theory including terms such as *tonic, dominant, sequence, interval,* etc.)

The composers appear chronologically according to their birthdates. Since some composers were child prodigies and others late bloomers, the list of composers does not necessarily represent a stylistic chronology. (Monteverdi, for instance, was born in the Renaissance but is mostly remembered for his innovations in the early Baroque style.) This guide does not claim to be comprehensive in its inclusion of all composers, especially concerning those active now in the twentieth and twenty-first centuries. Rather, the most famous names are listed, knowing that the reader will be competent to find sources that are more comprehensive to meet their needs when necessary. For the music appreciation student, I have marked (with an *) the composers most often discussed in the first-level music-history courses. The chapter of the book dealing with musical style relies on generalizations for the sake of understanding the musical periods and for comprehension of the overall picture of music history. Stylistic exceptions are not addressed in detail although the reader naturally will recognize their existence and importance.

It is the author's hope that readers will find this compact little source useful in their teaching, study, performance, and appreciation of music.

S.K. Murphy-Manley, 2004

A note about the second edition:

I would like to personally thank all of my students at Sam Houston State University for offering their valuable comments concerning the first edition. To the second edition I have added two new chapters: Chapter 5, *A Quick Survey of World Music* and Chapter 6, *A Quick Look at Jazz History*. These chapters are indeed, *quick*! They are useful, concise sources of summary information for which most students find themselves responsible these days. Additionally, I have added page numbers to the *List of Names with Dates*, (page 173) and a handy *Index of Terms*, (page 182).

Acknowledgments

I would like to thank Carol Smith for the impetus that created this resource book. I also want to thank the following people for their contribution to my general research and to this project: Rodney Cannon for his continued encouragement and support, Randy Adams, Wayne Barrett, Gerald Blakeman, Patricia Card, Barbara Corbin, Thomas Couvillon, Kathy Daniel, Peggy DeMers, Margaret Ferguson, Bruce Hall, Trent Hanna, Allen Hightower, Kristin Hightower, Henry Howey, Kyle Kindred, Mary Kay Lake, Matthew McInturf, Karen Epps Miller, Scott Philips, Scott Plugge, Sergio Ruiz, Alicia Tate, Jay Whatley, Andrew Wilson, Julie Schwab, and Nicole Alfred. I would like to offer special gratitude to Justin Nuckols and Sandra L. Murphy who gave generously of their time and research near the completion of the first edition of this book and to Terry Isgro who gave valuable input for the second edition.

I would also like to thank the following people on a personal level for their support: JohnMichael Manley, Sandra L. Murphy, Carter A. Manley, Charlene A. Huskey, Robert C. Murphy, Elma Stieben, Amy Graziano, John Stites, Clara Smith, and Mary Ann Lipsey.

I would also like to acknowledge and thank Sam Houston State University and The School of Music.

Introduction
Music history in a condensed melodic nutshell

As educators, most of us have had the experience of being asked to explain the life, music, and importance of a composer or musical time period in a limited amount of time. We all know that even semesters are too short to cover all of the relevant information concerning music history. I once was asked to present a ten-minute summary of Mozart's life *and* music to a performance class. Likewise, a summer music camp once required of me to discuss Medieval music (the entire 1500 years) in 15 minutes flat. I know that I am not alone in my experiences. Out of sheer desperation I developed the following statements to summarize the history of music in the smallest nutshell you've ever seen. I focused on the concept of melody, thus making these statements useful to the non-musician who usually has a clear understanding of melodies or tunes. As the reader can imagine, this small nutshell contains blatant generalizations that are not applicable to all of our surviving music. But, for the sake of speedy summarization, I have found the following quite useful.

If we examine the role that melody plays in the function of music throughout the years, we can help draw stylistic conclusions about the musical style in a particular time period and the purpose that music has served in our Western culture.

- In the Middle Ages (ca. 476-1420s) melody is used to convey *words* and express them in a very modest manner. The spotlight is aimed at the text and most composers are poets.

- In the Renaissance (1430-1600) melodies become numerous. Many melodies are played or sung simultaneously (polyphony) and therefore the words and the melodies themselves often are obscured. Because of this obscurity, the goal of music moves toward creating an effect on the listener.

- In the Baroque (1600-1730s/50) melody is used to express a particular mood, (usually one mood per piece or large section of music). These moods (emotions or affects) are *generic* feelings of joy, sorrow, rage, delight, etc., and not personalized (yours or mine). They are "basic human" emotions and not that of the composer. Rather, melodic fragments (motives) emerge to represent certain emotions. This music, with formulized emotions, is intended to arouse the same generic "universal" feeling in the listener.

- In the Classic Period (1730s-1810s) melody is used to establish symmetrical forms. Melody becomes the organizer of the musical composition and this results in frequent cadences and clear, symmetrical (even) phrasing. Music is polite, restrained, and ordered.

▲ In the Nineteenth Century (Romantic Period, 1810s-1900) melody is used to express the composer's feelings. Melodies become expansive, asymmetrical, and more expressive than ever before.

▲ In the Twentieth Century (1900-2000) melody is considered optional and often is abandoned in favor of atonality and asymmetry. Often there is no tonality, so there is no harmonic structure in which a melody can grow or even exist. By the 1970s, melodies are once again favored.

A Concise and Friendly Guide to Music History

Chapter 1

CR

An Overview of the Musical Elements in Each Historical Period

The elements of music are usually defined as melody, rhythm, harmony, texture, form, dynamics, and timbre (the color of instrumentation or orchestration). These elements are the materials of music. A musician can discern the date of a particular piece of music by observing the details of some or all of these musical elements. Each musical period tends to have general characteristics in common, thus making it possible to identify and date musical compositions. Naturally, there are exceptions to all generalizations. In fact, when the exceptions become more frequent and widespread in a culture, then a new musical period usually ensues.

These following comments are generalized by historical period and are intended to help the reader grasp a broad understanding of the musical elements in each time period. First, the typical division of musical periods is listed below. Following the short list, each time period is examined in greater detail to reflect more clearly the changes in musical style.

General List of Historical Eras (Musical Time Periods)

Antiquity:	~ 500 B.C. to 470s A.D.
Medieval:	~ 476 A.D. to 1420s (476 marks the fall of Rome)
Renaissance:	1430-1600
Baroque:	1600-1730s /1750 (J.S. Bach died in 1750)
Classical Era:	1740s-1800 /1810s (Also called the Age of Enlightenment)
19th Century:	1810s-1900 (Also called the Romantic Period)
20th Century:	1900-2000 (We have yet to name this century)

But, Wait! First, a Review of Musical Texture
(Texture is . . . *How the Music Fits Together*)

Texture refers to the interweaving of the melodic and harmonic elements of music. There are four basic textures of music that we teach in first-year music literature classes:

1. Monophony
2. Polyphony
3. Homophony
4. Heterophony

1. **Monophony** is the simplest (and we believe the oldest) texture. Monophony consists of a single melody. Additionally:

    a. Singing in octaves is still monophonic

    b. Adding non-pitched percussion does not change the monophonic texture, because monophony refers to the melody, not the rhythm.

    c. The addition of a drone (a sustained, unchanging pitch) does not create a harmonic change to the texture in musical times periods that did not recognize chords in the first place. (i.e. Ancient and Medieval music)

2. **Polyphony** developed in the 800s A.D. as organum.[1] Polyphony is the sounding of two or more melodies simultaneously. It is a texture based on counterpoint. There are actually two types of polyphony.

    Type 1: Two or more different melodies sounding simultaneously.

    Type 2: The same melody sounding at different times.

    > Type 2 is called *imitative polyphony*. A fugue is the epitome of counterpoint, and specifically, of imitative polyphony. Imitation is defined as the statement of a single melody or motive by two or more players or singers in succession, each taking turns with the "entrances" of the melody or motive. (If that sounds confusing, read the example and you will see that it is not.)
    >
    > *Example*: The melody, "Row, row, row your boat" is sung at different times, creating a round. This is called imitative polyphony. The imitation in a round is exact, but need not be in order to qualify as imitation. Childhood rounds are examples of *strict* imitation.

3. **Homophony** developed later than polyphony, becoming popular around 1600, the beginning of the Baroque. Homophony consists of a melody with an accompaniment. This accompaniment can be either:

    1. Chordal and rhythmically in sync with the melody (thus producing homorhythm), or
    2. The rhythm can be different, as in an accompanimental figure in a song.

---

[1] See Chapter 3, *Genres*, number 30.

A good example of the chordal sort of homophony is found in a typical Protestant hymn or carol. Think of your favorite hymn or carol and imagine that you are singing the alto or tenor part instead of the melody. You have just been singing part of this chordal accompaniment.

A good example of the sort of homophony with an accompanimental figure is a popular tune from a Broadway musical from the 1950s or 60s. In this case, there is a melody with a simple accompaniment that "plays" along with the singer. Both types of homophony are still favored in our American culture today.

Homorhythm Addressed:

We must mention a point concerning chordal homophony versus homorhythm. Homorhythm is created when two or more voices move in essentially the same rhythm, such as in a hymn or carol. But, music can be homorhythmic without being homophonic. How? Well, in order to have homophony, one needs functional tonality with a clear system of chordal progressions. Without this, homophony is not present . . . .

So, music can move in a homorhythmic texture without actually being homophonic or chordal. *Example*: Let's say that I take the tune "The Star-Spangled Banner" and change all of the rhythms to match the rhythms in the tune, "America the Beautiful". Then, let's say I have a band, choir, or orchestra play or sing this concoction. The rhythms are the same, but the "melody with accompaniment" is not present. In fact, it is polyphony—the simultaneous sounding of two melodies, even though the rhythms have been changed to match one another, resulting in homorhythm. So, in this example, we would have homorhythmic polyphony. [Discant organum is an example of this sort of musical texture.]

---

4. **Heterophony** consists of a melody that is accompanied by an embellished version of itself. And, by an "embellished version" one means more than merely "ornamented". This texture was popular in the Middle Ages and again in the 20th century.

    Example: Imagine that one singer is singing a very academic version of "Amazing Grace" while at the same time a competent pop-star is singing a different, embellished version, weaving in and out of the straight-laced singer's melody. The listener then hears a melody with an elaborately embellished version of itself sounding simultaneously. This is heterophony.

Okay— back to the descriptions of musical style.

Stylistic Comments in Greater Detail by Era

I. Antiquity (~ 500 B.C. to ~ 470s A.D.)[2]

Summary

- ⋏ Currently, we have about 45 musical pieces from this era and most of them are fragments. The music of antiquity was often transmitted aurally and improvisation played an important role. This might be one explanation for the very few extant fragments. These 45 pieces make up the Greek repertoire of Antiquity. No notated music survives from the Roman culture, although we know from written accounts that they had a flourishing culture.

- ⋏ The majority of the 45 examples of music that we have are in some way associated with dance, theater, or poetry.

- ⋏ Ancient vocal music was a fusion of rhythm, text, and melody (the latter of which Plato actually called harmony—but not meaning what we think of as harmony).

- ⋏ Music played a central role in civic and religious ceremonies. The mere 45 extant pieces do not reflect this accurately.

- ⋏ Pythagoras created a theory of music and mathematical relationship. The intervals of the octave (with a ratio of 2 to 1 using a divided string), the fifth (with a ratio of 3 to 2), and the fourth (with a ratio of 4 to 3) were the only three recognized consonances in ancient music. Thirds and sixths were out of tune in their tuning system and thus considered dissonances.

- ⋏ Music theorists believed that these three consonant intervals were linked with motions in the universe and states of the human soul.

- ⋏ For the ancients, music could affect an individual, for good or bad, and affect his behavior for or against the good of society. Much is written about the importance of hearing the "right kind" of music in order to be the "right kind" of man. Certain rhythms and modes were considered better suited for particular states (courage, melancholy, rage, etc). Some modes (think scales or keys) were considered vulgar and were to be avoided.

- ⋏ The Greek word for music, *mousike*, indicated a union of melody, rhythm, and text. The ancient musicians did not have an understanding of our specific word, *music*, nor of our notion of poetry that is merely read.

---

[2] For details, consult *The New Harvard Dictionary of Music* or the article on "Greece" in *The New Grove Dictionary of Music and Musicians.*

A. Melody

From the surviving 45 fragments[3] we can observe that melodies were created from the Greek musical system that was based on four interlocking tetrachords, (descending successions of four notes that span the interval of a fourth). These interlocking tetrachords created the Greater Perfect System. One of the best discussions of the ancient theorists Pythagoras and Aristoxenus in particular, is in the article by Thomas J. Mathiesen on *Greece*, in volume 10 of 2001 edition *The New Grove Dictionary of Music and Musicians*. Mathiesen also offers descriptions of the surviving *melos* (melodies) from this era.

The Greek system was complex with different scales and compositional procedures, and each "note" had at least two names, neither of which were the names we give notes today (A, C#, Do, Fa, etc).

Melodies were more conjunct in motion than disjunct. Some melodic motives were used in repetition, but the surviving melodies mostly appear to be more through-composed.[4] The melodies had a strong sense of tonic (called *mese*) and composers were encouraged to return to this tonic often in their tunes.[5]

B. Rhythm

It appears that rhythm was governed largely by the accents and metres of Greek poetry. If this is so, then the music was a combination of long and short values. This sort of arrangement also governs the rhythmic modes that emerge in the Middle Ages. Since a lot of this music from antiquity was virtuosic, it is obvious that there are things about its rhythm that we just do not know yet.

C. Harmony

For the most part, harmony was limited to occasional intervallic relationships of 4ths, 5ths, and octaves. (*Intervallic* means that only intervals are created, not chords. *Intervallic* means, merely the distance between two notes.) Greek musical theory does not appear to have recognized the "chord" as we know it today.

D. Texture

We believe that ancient music was predominantly monophonic.[6] When voices and instruments were used simultaneously, they sounded in unison or in octaves. It is possible that consonant drones were used (long, held notes at the interval of a 4th, 5th, or octave), but we have no supporting evidence that instruments had their own independent melodic or accompanimental line within vocal music. We believe that ancient Greek melodies were sometimes performed in a heterophonic manner. (Remember, this means that a melody was accompanied by a more ornate, embellished version of itself.)

---

[3] As of Spring 2006 these fragments could be heard on the website: http://www.oeaw.ac.at/kal/ agm/

[4] See Chapter 4, *Forms*, number 24.

[5] Mark Evan Bonds, *A History of Music in Western Culture* (Upper Saddle River: Prentice Hall, 2003), p. 6-7.

[6] For a review of textures, turn to page 2.

E. Form

The surviving examples we have are mostly through-composed, meaning that there are no large repetitions of music. The pieces could have been strophic with several stanzas of poetry in some cases. Future research may give us more understanding of the 45 examples that we have to study.

F. Dynamics

We can only speculate concerning the dynamics that were possible on the surviving instruments that we have recovered. Stringed instruments, by nature, are not loud. The aulos, we believe, was. If there are indications of dynamics on the surviving 45 fragments, they have not been deciphered.

G. Timbre

The timbre of the aulos was, by most accounts, partly nasal and strong. Stringed instruments would have been more subdued as were the blown pipes. We have an account by the statesman and poet Cicero (106-43 B.C.) concerning his opinion on the timbre of the Roman hydraulic organ that was powered by water pressure. He compared the sound of the organ to that of "fine food" and he associated it with "the most sensual feelings."[7]

H. Instruments

Stringed instruments were popular in antiquity. The *kithara*, the *lyre* is a simpler type, was so popular that kithara players (*kitharodes*) held concerts and competitions. We believe that the instruments either were plucked with the fingers or a plectrum (think "pick"). The lyre and the kithara both were built in many different sizes, some of which received individual names, such as the *barbitos*, a type of lyre with a lower range. *Harps* were also popular and came in various sizes and shapes, too.

The *aulos* was the most popular wind instrument during antiquity. In the 20th century, it was commonly mistranslated as "flute" which it was not. It was a reed instrument (it might have been a single or double reed) with three to five holes, and played in a vertical (recorder-like fashion) that was loud enough to have been used on a battlefield as iconographical evidence demonstrates. We have drawings of musicians playing two aulos simultaneously, suggesting that a drone might have been used. (We really are unsure.) Additionally, there were other pipe-like instruments that could be considered precursors to the flute. Organs were also constructed of pipes and they used wind to activate the various pitches. The hydraulic organ in Roman culture was especially popular and used in civic ceremonies and competitions. Brass wind instruments included the Roman *cornu* (curved horn) and the *serpent* (trumpet). Brass instruments were usually used for signals. In Greece, the straight trumpet (*salpinx*) and the curved horn (*keras*) were also used in battle.

Percussion instruments were apparently commonly used. We know of tambourines (*tympana*), finger cymbals (*kumbala*), hollowed-out blocks (*krotala*), and rattles (*sistrum*).

---

[7] Bonds, p. 8.

II. Middle Ages / Medieval Period (~ 476 A.D. to 1420s)

Summary

⋏ Music of the Medieval Period was largely functional, serving its purpose in religious services, courting, weddings, civic ceremonies, dancing, and entertaining.

⋏ Both the notation of pitch and rhythm developed during this time, pitch first. Notation began to be used in the 9th century, but we cannot transcribe it properly until the 11th century.

⋏ The church was the primary institution for musical production.

⋏ Most instrumental accompaniments to monophonic songs were largely improvised.

⋏ Composers rarely specified instruments or vocal forces in their manuscripts.

⋏ Today, general descriptions of Medieval music often concentrate on the absence of musical features that become understood in the Renaissance, such as the use of counterpoint as a compositional technique and the concept of a harmonic organization of the music.

⋏ By the end of the period, compositional practices became drastically complex compared to the earlier use of mere monophonic melodies. These developments opened the door widely to new compositional methods for future composers.

A. Melody

Melodies of the Middle Ages were mostly conjunct and usually were confined to the range (*ambitus*) of a sixth or an octave. Music was based on the system of the eight church modes (Dorian, Hypodorian, Phrygian, Hypophrygian, Lydian, Hypolydian, Mixolydian, and Hypomixolydian). *Melismas* (extended passages of several notes set to one syllable of text) were common and employed in many genres.

B. Rhythm

It is only fair to believe that some of the secular songs sung in the Middle Ages were sung in a rhythm to a more or less steady beat. Likewise, instrumental music for dancing, and the rhythmic nature that movement implies, called for rhythmic regularity. In the 12th century (1100s), rhythmic modes were devised by composers to help them notate rhythm. These modes were used until the 13th century. The notation did not show fixed relative durations with note symbols. Rather, the rhythmic modes showed rhythmic patterns by using certain combinations of single neumes and neume groups (or longs and shorts). By 1250 the rhythmic modes were codified as the six modes and identified by number. The rhythmic patterns sound to our modern ears as 6/8 patterns, corresponding to metrical feet of French and Latin poetry (trochee, iamb, dactyl, anapest).

Below are the six Medieval rhythmic modes.

I. ♩ ♪   IV. ♪ ♩ ♩.

II. ♪ ♩   V. ♩. ♩.

III. ♩. ♪ ♩   VI. ♪ ♪ ♪

C. Harmony

The system of harmony and its chordal structure was not invented yet. But, in polyphony, intervals of the 4th, 5th, and the octave were still favored as consonances. The intervals of the second and seventh were widely used, while the intervals of the third and sixth were avoided. Medieval harmony was a result of polyphonic texture, not of chords. (Note: At the end of the Middle Ages, thirds and sixths became popular and this new style actually became the Renaissance style.)

D. Texture

Most music from the <u>early Middle Ages</u> was monophonic in texture. This means that only one line of music existed. This melody was not accompanied by any significant harmony or other melodic figure. Some music in the Middle Ages was performed in a heterophonic texture. We believe that some melodies, especially those in the secular genre, were accompanied by an improvised drone or rhythmic figure. This improvisation did not change the monophonic texture.

By the <u>middle</u> and <u>end</u> of the <u>Medieval period</u>, three and four-part polyphonic textures were common. This new polyphony was the most significant advancement in musical style. For the first time in music history, composition becomes a skill and an art.

E. Form

In the Middle Ages, text and poetic form determined the musical structure of melodies and compositions. In other words, one finds genres in the Middle Ages that are poetic forms of the day, (ballades, lais, rondeaux, virelais, madrigals, etc.).

F. Dynamics

We do not know much about the dynamics used in the Middle Ages. One suspects that the loud and soft instruments governed the volume of the music. We do know that the technique of singing was different than our modern use of the voice, but scholars are in dispute as to the exact nature of the difference. Many believe that the singing had a more nasal, forward quality.

G. Timbre (orchestration)

We know very little about the combinations of instruments used with and without voices, because we have so few indications of composers' intentions. We do understand that vocal polyphony in the church was reserved for soloists while choruses were responsible for singing monophonic melodies.

H. Instruments[8]

Some of the stringed instruments popular in the Middle Ages include the harp, lute, lyre, organistrum, psaltery, vielle, and the viol. By the end of the Medieval Period, the lute was very popular, and stringed ensembles of viols of various sizes were common.

Organs of various sizes were also common. Grand or great organs were large organs built inside churches. A portative organ was small enough to be carried or placed on a table. A positive organ was a larger organ usually without pedals. The sounds of all the organs were produced by wind blowing through pipes. Another wind instrument that utilized pipes was the bagpipe, which later became a folk instrument.

Other wind instruments included recorders of all sizes, traverse flutes (flutes held horizontally when played), shawms (piercing double-reed woodwinds, popular in various sizes, from 1200 to around 1600) and brass instruments including horns and trumpets of several types.

III. Ars Nova / Trecento (1300-1350)

Summary

⊿ The primary change in musical style during the first half of the 14th century concerned rhythm. The term, *Ars nova*, meant the new *art*, *technique*, or *craft*, as opposed to the older 13th century style, *Ars antiqua*.

⊿ The *Ars nova* refers to the new style in France, while the *trecento* refers to the new style in Italy.

⊿ The first collection of ars nova music dates from 1316. The collection, called the *Roman de Fauvel*, is actually a long poem by Gervais du Bus (a French author and writer) that is interspersed with more than 100 monophonic and polyphonic musical pieces.

⊿ Aspects of the music from the Ars nova include complexity, sometimes extreme, of rhythm (with polymeters and polyrhythms), freer use of striking dissonances of 2nds and 7ths, and a newer singing style that was considered by Jacques de Liège in 1324/5 to be lascivious.

⊿ Philippe de Vitry's treatise from ca. 1322/3, called *Ars nova*, discussed some of the more modern techniques.

---

[8] See *The New Grove Dictionary of Musical Instruments*, edited by Stanley Sadie, London: Macmillan Press, 1984, for a complete and detailed history of all instruments.

⮝ The modern aspects of this new art included the following:
  1. A compositional technique of musical organization called isorhythm
  2. A compositional technique that enlivened the music called hocket
  3. The rhythmic division of the "beat" into two equal parts (instead of the older division of three)
     — The triple division of the beat (think of a dotted whole note equaling three half notes) was called *tempus perfectum*
     — The new, more controversial, duple division of the beat (think two dotted half notes equaling one dotted whole note) was called *tempus imperfectum*
     — What resulted were four "meters" equivalent to our modern time signatures of 6/8, 9/8, 3/4, and 2/4
  4. The use of more varied rhythms outside of the older six rhythmic modes
  5. New notation was created to reflect these changes in the rhythm

IV. Renaissance (1430-1600)

Summary

⮝ In 1477, the theorist, Johannes Tinctoris in his *Liber de arte contrapuncti*, announced a rebirth in the art of music. He claimed that the founders of this newer, consonant style were Dufay and Binchois, with the English, namely John Dunstable taking the lead.

⮝ The striking dissonances and complexities of the Ars nova were abandoned in favor of parallel 3rds and 6ths. An English style of Fauxbourdon emerged and was favored for its beauty and consonance.

⮝ When composers from mainland Europe heard this new Renaissance style they called it, joyous, brilliantly consonant, and very pleasing.

⮝ Secular music took an equal place alongside sacred music.

⮝ Vocal music still dominated and a cappella vocal polyphony achieved its greatest perfection during the Renaissance.

⮝ Word-painting became a technique that was used to help express and present the meaning of a text. (For instance, if the text was "ascend," the vocal line might rise through a scale.)

⮝ Musical notation began a process of standardization, but did not achieve it fully until the Baroque.

⮝ Courts, along with churches, were the institutions in which musical production flourished.

A. Melody

The melodies of Renaissance music were for the most part, flowing and melismatic in nature. The melodies used wider leaps for the expression of the text but were more still conjunct than disjunct. The top voice often became the bearer of the melodic material, but when melodies were numerous in the polyphony, a vague quality of melodic distinction existed. On the other hand, some genres contained a sung melody in the top voice accompanied by subservient instrumental melodies below, thus highlighting the melodic line.

Secular tunes (and sacred ones, too) often were used as the basis of sacred compositions. When these pre-existing melodies were placed in a new piece they were called *cantus firmi* (plural of a *cantus firmus*). This practice began by using a plainchant as the cantus firmus, but became an uncontrolled compositional delight through which sacred music and secular music began to intermingle. In the 1540s, the Catholic Church called for reforms and asked composers to stop using secular tunes in their sacred music.

B. Rhythm

Rhythm in the Renaissance lost most of its complexity. Triple and duple groupings were used side-by-side as dictated by the text. The rhythms of Renaissance music were largely simple compared to those in the ars nova and to those in the Baroque period that followed.

C. Harmony

Harmony in the Renaissance began to focus on progressions of 3rds and 6ths. Chordal textures resulted in complete triads, although this sort of harmonic foundation was not yet a topic of discussion for composers. Dissonances were discouraged, and consonances were preferred. When dissonances were used, they were prepared and resolved.

The harmonic structure of Renaissance music was still based on the church modes. And, although some music may have used altered modes that resulted in major or minor keys, the major/minor key system did not develop until the Baroque. So, the tonal system of the Renaissance was modality.

D. Texture

Three and four-part polyphonic works were the norm in the beginning of the Renaissance. By the 16th century, five to eight voices were the norm and experimentations of excess became popular. (Thomas Tallis' *Spem in alium* is a motet composed for 40 voices, 8 choirs of 5 voices each.) A balance of stylistic equality among the musical parts characterized the Renaissance style and a cappella vocal polyphony dominated sacred music.

Homorhythm was fairly common in both instrumental and vocal music. (The *Credo* from Josquin's *Missa Pange lingua* is actually an early example of homophony. But, this texture is an exception and Josquin was ahead of his time when he composed this chorale-like mass movement.) One often found an alternation of homorhythm and polyphony within one work, thus giving the composition a formal structure of musical divisions.

Counterpoint became the Renaissance composer's primary technique while imitative counterpoint developed in 1476 through Josquin, becoming a favored texture in the 16th century. Additional contrapuntal techniques developed including augmentation, diminution, retrograde, and inversion. Canons became popular and widely published.

E. Form

Masses were controlled greatly by the use of a cantus firmus. Madrigals emerged in the 1540s as the new modern genre and the forms were largely poetic. Strophic forms in popular music were common. Many musical forms were still dictated by their poetic structures. Binary forms became common in instrumental music.

F. Dynamics

The practice of *cori spezzati* (one larger choir broken into two smaller ones) created a situation in which the larger, loud group was contrasted with the smaller, softer group. Instruments were characterized as either *haut* or *bas*, (loud or soft). Actual dynamic markings first appeared in lute literature in the early 1500s.

G. Timbre (orchestration)

We know that by Josquin's time, choirs were beginning to be used in the performance of vocal polyphony. Philip the Good, duke of Burgundy from 1419 to 1467 left us significant documentation of his musical entourage. In addition to the musicians in his chapel he maintained a group of minstrels including, trumpeters, drummers, viellists, lutenists, harpists, organists, bagpipers, and shawm players. For mass, which was sung everyday, he used six trebles, three tenors, two bass contras, two middle contras, and four chaplains. He was an amateur musician and great patron of the arts so his collection of musicians should be considered unusual.

We can conclude that the timbre of Renaissance music became more varied than ever before with new combinations of instruments and singers. Interestingly, however, the uniformity of sounds within ensembles of singers, stringed instruments, recorders, or brass instruments, was still desired.

H. Instruments

The loud (haut) instruments were shawms, cornets (hollowed-out wood instruments with finger holes and a brass-like mouthpiece), slide trumpets and sackbuts (predecessors of trombones).

The soft (bas) instruments included harps, vielles, lutes, psalteries, portative organs, traverse flutes, and recorders.

Percussion instruments included kettledrums, bells of various sorts, and cymbals.

During the late Renaissance the harpsichord and clavichord rose in popularity and there was a new repertoire of keyboard music that emerged.

V. Early Baroque (1600-1650)

Summary

⅄ Some of the most significant changes in musical style occurred around 1600, including the development of functional tonality as reflected in our modern major/minor key system. This tonal development took about 100 years, but its formal beginnings were in the early Baroque.

⅄ A new bass line, basso continuo, created a harmonic foundation in compositions making the rise of homophony extraordinary.[9]

⅄ Opera was invented in Florence, Italy. Recitative and monody were the central components of expression in opera and in other solo vocal music of the early Baroque. Monody (a single melodic line with basso continuo accompaniment that was essentially a solo song) came about as a reaction against Renaissance polyphony.

⅄ Secular art music became more important than it ever had been in the Middle Ages.

⅄ The idea that every piece, or every movement, should convey a predominate emotion or mood began to create a new Baroque aesthetic. This notion was referred to as the *Doctrine of Affections*. These emotions, or *passions*, were not personal expressions of the composer, but rather generic human emotions that performers hoped to arouse in their audience. Discussions of the *imitation* of emotion (or nature) ensued in theoretical treatises.

⅄ Performers became important ambassadors of these new emotions and affects.

⅄ Courts and churches together were the primary institutions for musical production. The two institutions began to compete for the best composers and musicians.

⅄ There was a coexistence of the older, first practice (*prima prattica*) and the newer (*seconda prattica*) practice (think style). The new homophonic style of writing did not replace counterpoint. Thus, Baroque music became more varied in texture than music in the Renaissance had been.

A. Melody

The melody in homophony became the most expressive device in music. And, the most expressive melodic device in the early Baroque was *recitative*. Recitative was the central emotional component of early operas. Interestingly, recitative is not very melodic in nature, but rather it is a style of text setting that emphasizes the natural rhythms and accents of speech (Remember, the first operas were in Italian). The pitch range was usually confined and there was limited repetition of words. This homophonic recitative was the new style of melodic declamation that was believed, in 1600, to be the supreme vehicle for textual and emotional expression.

Virtuosity became important to musical performance. Soloists, both vocal and instrumental, were provided opportunities to display shows of brilliance and

---

[9] See page 95 for an explanation of basso continuo.

expression. Improvisation played an important role concerning the ornamentation of melodic lines.

B. Rhythm

In the early 17th century, rhythms were performed more freely in recitative. There was a special expressive quality that was desired in the music, especially in vocal music. Instrumental music continued some of its association with dance and the theater. A large repertoire of keyboard music emerged with rhythms more modern and complex than those found in the Renaissance. Eventually, certain rhythmic motives became common and were associated with particular affections (emotions).

C. Harmony

In the early Baroque there was a shift from modality to tonality. By 1700, tonality was dominated by the diatonic scale and the 24 major and minor keys. Since a lute can easily be tuned in any desired method, the functional idea of these 24 keys took root in lute literature first.

While Renaissance composers considered harmony to be a byproduct of counterpoint, (a horizontal aspect of the music), the composers of the Baroque began to think of harmony in regards to chordal progressions, (a vertical process). Our part-writing exercises in music school are based on this vertical concept.)

D. Texture

Homophony was the new texture that changed the nature of music around 1600. But, polyphony continued to flourish, especially the organized, skillful use of counterpoint and its devices.

E. Form

Many forms of vocal music continued to be determined by the poetic form of the text. Operatic subgenres (arias and recitatives) were often through-composed. Some strophic forms were used when the stanzas of text allowed it. Binary forms were still popular in instrumental music and variations became a novelty.

F. Dynamics

Dynamic markings of *piano* and *forte* came into general use in the 1600s in Italian music. We also know from theoretical writings that the terms, *echo* and *trill* were commonly used. Terraced dynamics (shifting from loud to soft without gradations) became popular.

G. Timbre (orchestration)

In the Baroque, contrasts of timbre were cultivated. By the end of the Baroque, the main component of musical composition, in general, was contrast. Large groups were contrasted against small groups, soft groups against loud, and high instruments against low ones. Eventually, dialogue-style writing between voices and strings, or strings and winds, became popular.

H. Instruments

During the Baroque era many improvements were made to stringed instruments and to organs. In fact, the Baroque became the golden age of the organ, and technical improvements to the harpsichord would eventually give way to the invention of the piano in the 18th century. The oboe emerged in the early 17th century as a successor to the shawm. The bassoon, too, emerged during this time and was used primarily as a basso continuo instrument.

VI. Middle Baroque (1650-1700)

Summary

▲ In the Mid-Baroque, counterpoint was cultivated in instrumental genres resulting in fugues, chaccones, and passacaglias.

▲ Instrumental music took a new lead creating new genres such as concertos, sonatas, and trios.

▲ Italian opera spread throughout Europe and developed into a more defined organization of alternating recitatives and arias.

▲ Ballets were very popular in France.

▲ Secular and sacred music existed side-by-side, and secular music eventually takes the lead.

▲ Churches and courts remained the most important avenues for music making.

▲ In 1637, Venice opened the first public opera house in the world. This new establishment created a business-like atmosphere for operas and stage productions. This created a new venue for public entertainment.

A. Melody

By the middle of the Baroque the recitative melodies gave way to more lyrical *bel canto* arias and solo songs. Melodies became more clearly organized with the use of compositional techniques such as repetition, sequence, and contrast. The phrases were still dictated by the text, but a virtuosic aspect began to create melodic lines that were more instrumentally conceived. (In layman's terms, the melodies sounded more like melodies.)

B. Rhythm

Rhythm became a central element in instrumental music. The basso continuo gave music a rhythmic drive, especially in the faster pieces. Dotted rhythms, such as in a French overture, were quite common in a variety of genres. Melodies were created around the sixteenth-note rhythm for vitality. Dance rhythms were also important in Mid-Baroque music.

C. Harmony

The tonal system of our 24 major and minor keys continued to develop.

D. Texture

Both homophony and polyphony were commonly used.

E. Form

The most important developments in form began to occur in the late 17th century. Fugues developed out of an obsession with imitation, rhetoric, and organization. Da capo arias developed from an obsession with the human voice as an expression of emotion and an increasing desire to witness virtuosic feats. The notion of a return (think recapitulation) became the predominating factor to the formal organization of music. Ritornellos were used in concertos and in arias as the main musical idea (think theme) that returned throughout a piece.

F. Dynamics

The notion of crescendoing and decrescendoing was understood, but not marked very often. Terraced dynamics were still preferred.

G. Timbre (orchestration)

As the tuning system began to change to accommodate the diatonic system of keys, so did the timbre of instruments. Ensembles were still small (compared to our notions of an orchestra today) and the music would have been a more "quiet" event than we might think. We can assume that the tuning system, since it was not like our own today, gave the music a different color. If we were to hear it today, we might think it sounded "out-of-tune."

H. Instruments

Stringed instruments dominated instrumental music. In fact, strings dominated in the accompanimental parts in vocal music, too. (Let's just say, that at this point in history, strings dominated ensemble music and would continue to do so until the 19th century.) In the late 17th century, there were ensembles of strings that were merely complimented with pairs of winds, usually, flutes, oboes, bassoons, trumpets, and horns. The basso continuo group still was the foundation of musical production. Harpsichords, clavichords, and organs were the primary keyboard instruments. Since most pieces used a basso continuo, most Baroque music used a harpsichord or an organ, (or sometimes a lute).

VII. Late Baroque (1700–1730s/50)

<u>Summary</u>

⚞ By the late Baroque, instrumental music rose further in significance and importance.

   ↟ Serious opera, heroic opera that was called, *opera seria*, was the primary form of public musical entertainment.

   ↟ Public concerts emerged as a new venture for composers, performers, and impresarios.

   ↟ The successes of opera brought about the successes of castrati and other virtuosic performers. Composers competed for the best singers to perform their new operas in hopes of multiple performances and new commissions.

   ↟ Composers' livelihoods depended on commissions from courts and public venues.

   ↟ The court was the primary patron of the arts.

   ↟ Churches offered composers and performers steady jobs in music production and teaching duties, but the money to be made was in opera.

   ↟ The doctrine of affections created an idiomatic style of composition.

   ↟ Seventh chords were accepted as functional harmony.

A. Melody

Melodies were governed by "fortspinnung" (the spinning out of musical ideas) and sequences. Therefore, melodies were often long with a sense of continuous development moving toward a cadence or stopping point. Melodic phrases, consequently, were not always clearly defined. Virtuosity was important as was the improvisation of ornaments and embellishments, especially on repeated sections of music.

B. Rhythm

The basso continuo rhythmically and metrically drove the music. As far as we know, the tempos were mostly steady in ensemble music. The late Baroque was the era of the sixteenth note and the notation of music was standardized for these rhythms that were formulaic and regular.

C. Harmony

By the 1720s the modern diatonic system of 24 major and minor keys was finally firmly established. Chromaticism was used for expression, modulation, and musical interest. (For instance, a descending chromatic line represented grief.) The harmonic rhythm (the speed at which the music changes to and from each chord) was rapid, with chords changing several times in every measure. Basic triads and inversions were common with some use of 7ths.

D. Texture

Polyphony began to represent the serious or "learned" church style, while homophony was the language of the modern style.

E. Form

The da capo aria form was the most popular vocal form, and ritornello form was the most popular "orchestral," or ensemble, form. Fugues still ruled contrapuntal music. Binary forms were common in dance movements and sonatas.

F. Dynamics

By the early 1700s, hairpins (crescendo and decrescendo markings) were used in Paris and London and in Italian music. In the 1740s in Mannheim, Johann Stamitz made the orchestral crescendo a sensation, creating a new demand for dynamics in instrumental music.

G. Timbre (orchestration)

The notion of an "orchestra" began to take shape as Sammartini invented the symphony in Milan in the 1730s and 40s. The new genre (symphony) is a classic genre, but having its roots in the Baroque era, it was originally performed with a basso continuo. A new orchestral virtuosity emerged in Mannheim in the 1740s with Johann Stamitz's orchestra of phenomenal musicians. He and his orchestra changed the history of orchestral timbre to one of strength.

H. Instruments

Continued experimentations with the construction of the keyboard leads to the emergence of pianoforte prototypes. Stringed instruments were still the primary sections in all ensembles. Virtuosos on the violin, flute and oboe began to make successful careers as well. By this time, bassoons were not limited to the basso continuo part, although they often played it. Recorders were still prominent and a marking of *flauto* in a Baroque manuscript indicated a recorder. Traverse (sometimes written, *transverse*) flutes were used, too, and were usually called *flauto traverso* in scores.

VIII. The Galant Style (1730s-1760s)

Summary

⋏ The galant style was the beginning of the classic style.

⋏ These early classic traits used to be called "pre-classic". We do not use this term anymore because of the inferior connotation.

⋏ Changes included a simplification of all of the musical elements and their use.

⋏ *Empfindsamkeit* is a German term (meaning literally, "to feel sentimental") associated with this change in style.

⋏ Galant music lost the rhythmic drive of the Baroque and replaced it with an enlightened, noble negligence of strong emotion.

⅄ It seems that with the new modern classic style, complications associated with the art of music relaxed, took a step backward, and then simplified in search of simplistic beauty.

A. Melody

The galant melody became simple and symmetrical. The melodies were easily sung and lyrical in nature. The notion of fortspinnung was abandoned in favor of antecedent and consequent phrase structure. This structure created two-part phrases that were symmetrical. Cadences were regular as a result of the clear and even phrasing. Melody became the primary focus.

B. Rhythm

Rhythms of galant music became less formulaic. Ornaments complicated the rhythms that were used in slower, sentimental movements. Dances and their rhythmic feel influenced galant and classic music to a great extent.[10]

C. Harmony

The most notable change in harmony was the slowing down of the harmonic rhythm. In galant music, entire measures, or even groups of measures, dwelled on only one chord, while Baroque music used several chord changes in each measure. Chromaticism was used for emotional affect, but most emotional displays were restrained. Accompanimental figures were favored above the more difficult bass lines of the Baroque basso continuo. In fact, basso continuo, began to be discontinued. In galant music it was not uncommon for the bass line to drop out for several measures at a time, giving the music a more delicate, "enlightened" sense. Harmonically, composers became obsessed with the relationship between the dominant and tonic keys. Most music was organized harmonically in a very clear and deliberate manner.

D. Texture

Since melody was the focus of galant music, the favored texture was homophony. Counterpoint was still popular, but in church music.

E. Form

Sonata form and dance forms predominated music from the mid 18th century. Forms were clearly defined by a juxtaposition of the tonic and dominant keys. Even phrases were often arranged according to this tonic/dominant relationship.

F. Dynamics

Forte and *piano* contrasts were still the norm. Crescendos and decrescendos were used, but not too frequently. Expressive markings, such as *dolce* became increasingly common.

---

[10] See Wye Allanbrook's *Rhythmic Gesture in Mozart: "Le Nozze di Figaro" and "Don Giovanni"*, 1983.

G. Timbre (orchestration)

The most significant change in the timbre of galant music was the lessening importance of the basso continuo line. Performances of the new repertoire of symphonies included a harpsichord from which the composer often directed the ensemble.

H. Instruments

Stringed instruments continued to dominate. As the second half of the 18th century approached, more usable prototypes of the pianoforte began to emerge. By the 1770s, a marketable, practical, version of the early piano was available. Keyboard music was especially suited to this new galant style. The clarinet appeared in the orchestra in Mannheim in the 1750s.

IX. The Classic Period (1740s-1810s)

Summary

⌃ All of the galant musical traits became the classic style. (See "The Galant Style")

⌃ Within this ordered, polite, and systematic music, an opposite emotional stylistic outburst emerged in the 1770s called *Sturm und Drang* (Storm and Stress). This style featured more emotional expression, which was, in one way, manifested by the use of more minor keys. This *Sturm und Drang* movement (founded originally in German literature) eventually led to Romanticism of the 19th century.

⌃ Sonata form experienced its highest achievements in the classic era.

⌃ Compositions became polythematic, desiring more than one main theme.

⌃ The classic style utilized repeated notes in melodic and accompanimental passages.

⌃ Occasional rests, or surprise stops, were used for effect.

⌃ The tempo was steady and regular with very little use of rubato in ensemble music.

⌃ Opera was the main form of public entertainment in the beginning of the period. But, by 1800, instrumental concerts began to rise in importance, rivaling operatic performances in the 19th century.

⌃ Humor could be created in music by playing on the expectations of the simple musical language of the time. Haydn was the most effective composer of wit.

⌃ Church music, in particular the arias, began to resemble the secular arias of the day. Castrati performed with great acclaim in churches and in theaters.

⌃ Courts and churches still provided composers and musicians with the most and best steady employment.

⌃ Composers strove for operatic commissions that brought about fame and income.

A. Melody
Melodies were singable and were created with symmetrical phrasing. Musical gestures of fanfare, brilliance, singing style, etc. emerged and dominated the musical syntax of the era.[11] Truly, music became a language in the 18th century, capable of expressing emotions and characterizations without text. Instrumental music, in particular, became a new avenue of musical expression. (This notion would be taken to its fullest potential in the 19th century.)

B. Rhythm
Rhythms were used as gestures, including those of the dance and fanfare. Rhythms were not complex, and seemed to exist to serve the melodic content.

C. Harmony
Harmonies remained predictable and uncomplicated. The harmonic rhythm was slow as in galant music. Development sections in sonata form utilized faster harmonic rhythms.

D. Texture
Homophony was the texture of choice unless a composer wanted to evoke religious, ceremonial, or serious topics. Then counterpoint or some form of polyphony was employed.

E. Form
Sonata form continued to rule the world of instrumental music.

Rondos were extremely popular as well. Ternary forms (in arias) indicated a modern style while the older da capo arias were associated with a more serious style.

F. Dynamics
Dynamics were an integral part of musical expression and composition in the Classic Era. Often *forte* and *piano* contrasts appeared several times within only one measure. Expressive markings began to increase in usage as well. Pianissimo and fortissimo markings were used sparingly, increasing in occurrence as the 19th century approached.

G. Timbre (orchestration)
The clarinet was added to the orchestral ensemble as a regular member, changing the sound of the wind section. Timpani were still used conservatively for effects in *forte* passages. The fortepiano added a new timbre to chamber and orchestral music.

---

[11] See Leonard Ratner's *Classic Music: Expression, Form, and Style*, 1980.

H. Instruments

A patented version of the piano emerged in England in 1777. From this point on, the piano experienced changes that strengthened it and expanded its versatility. By the 1770s and 80s the clarinet was commonly used in orchestral, as well as in chamber, music giving the composer a new tone color to manipulate.

X. Nineteenth Century / Romantic Period (1810s-1900)

Summary

▲ The 19th century saw some of the most radical changes to music since music's recorded history.

▲ Emotional content (and that of the composer's) was now the focus. Composers were expected to imbue their music with strong emotional content.

▲ Programmatic music became popular as a means of expressing dramatic situations and emotions without sung text.

▲ There was a desire for large, grand productions as well as the opposite desire for small intimate musical experiences. (i.e. large choral-orchestral works, versus a solo character piece for piano or a Lied for the salon)

▲ Romanticism had a peculiar obsession with individual feeling and an interest in the nature and mind of the artist.

▲ There was a desire to glorify feeling and passion over reflection and self-control.

▲ Emotions were "romanticized" (made larger than life) and deeply felt.

▲ The supernatural and macabre were topics that interested artists in the 19th century.

▲ Strange new harmonies (sounding sinister to a conservative listener) resulted from this desire to create the deepest-felt emotions.

▲ Artists began to distrust "rules" of composition (including harmony and form) and began creating new forms and new harmonic rules.

▲ New tone colors emerged when composers orchestrated passages for instruments never before combined. Additionally, the brass and percussion sections were enlarged. (This new and bold method of orchestration was one of the aspects of 19th-century music by which we can identify its style aurally.)

▲ Chromaticism was used freely.

▲ The practice of improvisation of trills and ornaments from the 18th century was discontinued.

▲ The tempo rubato (borrowed time) was constantly used creating the need for more conductors.

▲ Solo recitals became popular and widespread.

⅄ The patronage system all but disappeared. Courts were replaced by upper and upper-middle class patrons.

⅄ There were two schools of thought (we call them camps) in the 19th century. The conservative composers included Brahms, Schumann, and Mendelssohn –among others, and the more progressive camp included Wagner, Berlioz, and Liszt. They fought about everything.

A. Melody
Melodies could still be symmetrical, but for the most part, composers preferred to write more expansive and elongated musical thoughts. The upward leap of a sixth was the "romantic" interval, and many melodies included it, or even began with it. Melody was still a focal point for romantic composers, but the harmonic underlay of that melody was just as important to them and much more important than it had been to 18th century composers.

B. Rhythm
Beginning with Beethoven, heroicism in the 19th century became the 100-year fad. This resulted in a desire for fanfare-like musical statements in orchestral music. Dances lost their dominating force on rhythm that they previously held in the 18th century. Rhythm, partly because of the use rubato, took on a more free nature in the 19th century alongside the staunch heroic gestures. This music also utilized more meter changes than ever before.

C. Harmony
Remarkable advances occurred in the harmonic nature of music in the 19th century. Sevenths, ninths, and harmonic chromaticism dominated almost every genre of music. Wagner created the wildest innovations that would eventually lead to harmonic theories of the 20th century. Dissonance was used freely without "proper" preparation. Tonal progressions by thirds became popular and although the harmony of the 19th century was still functional, it moved to an extended tonal system by the end of the 1800s.

D. Texture
Homophony, polyphony, and monophony were all used in the 19th century. Texture was rarely the focus of expression, but instead, it was usually the servant of emotional display.

E. Form
Forms from the 18th century, such as sonata, variations, ritornello, and rondo, continued popularity in the 19th century but with expansions and additions. Conservative composers tended to cling to the classic or traditional compositional techniques, while the progressive composers sometimes abandoned them altogether.

F. Dynamics

In the 19th century, dynamics were used for the first time in music history to their fullest potential. As personal expression and emotional content became a focus, dynamics became central devices for the style. Never before in time does music experience such a wide array of expressions of volume, tempo, and mood.

G. Timbre (orchestration)

For the first time in music history, orchestration became an art form in itself. Berlioz innovated outrageous combinations of instruments and untraditional usages of traditional instruments as early as 1830. The progressive composers, in particular, made extraordinary changes in the expectations of the roles for various orchestral instruments. This eventually led to the unseating of the stringed instruments from their 200-year orchestral dominance. Orchestration treatises were published and studied.

H. Instruments

It is during the 19th century that most modern improvements were made to orchestral instruments. The piano received its most important improvements and the tuning of many instruments was significantly refined. Percussion instruments found an important voice in the progressive music of the century. Likewise, other instruments that had been considered "accompanying" instruments were able to throw off stereotypes and be integrated into the new modern orchestral sound.

XI. Twentieth Century (1900-2000)

Summary

▲ By the 20th century, music experienced the most varied and radical developments in its history.

▲ There was no one style or trend that dominated the century.

▲ The century began with drastic rebellions against past traditions (the 19th century in particular) and it ended with a return to many traditional elements and styles of all of music's past.

▲ Tonality was abandoned. and then redefined into neo-tonality (a new tonality, different than the one based on our 24 major and minor keys).

▲ Composers were fascinated with extremes: pitch range, dynamics, lengths, etc.

▲ Music frequently employed mixed meter and new ideas of rhythm. Some composers even created new unheard of rhythms and new notations to write them down. New instruments had to be created to play some of this new complex music.

▲ The new 20th-century harmonic innovations resulted from the intense chromaticism of the late 19th century.

▲ Polytonality, polyrhythms, polymeters, polychords, and even a return to older polyphonic techniques, all played an important role in the 20th century.

⮦ During the first half of the century, all things that were common to music were at some point abandoned. This included not only the musical elements that we have been discussing, but also the entire notion of what music was in the first place and what the concept of musical instruments even were.

⮦ During this time of drastic "rule-breaking" the world of tonal popular music began to emerge with the blues, ragtime, and jazz.

⮦ Music was redefined in the middle of the century to include all organized sound.

⮦ Eventually, even the need for organization was questioned.

⮦ New electronic instruments were developed that changed the history of musical composition and performance.

— Since so many traditional elements were abandoned in the 20th century, it will benefit us here to describe particular styles that found an audience in the 20th century.

- Two primary styles emerged in the early years of the century. Debussy introduced <u>Impressionism</u> in France in the 1890s. This style held on to many musical elements while abandoning the traditional rules for each. In particular, the rules of chord progression were abandoned and all *chords* were treated equally.

- <u>Expressionism</u> emerged in Germany with Schoenberg leading the way. In this modern style, all twelve *notes* were treated equally and the notion of tonality, or of having a tonal center, was abandoned.

I. Impressionism

- Melody was still an important element of Impressionism, but the melodies did not need to follow traditional expectations of inception, growth, and resolution. A melody could be randomly placed and be out of context in the musical structure of the work.

- The one overriding trait of Impressionism was the vague quality of each of the musical elements. (In Impressionist paintings the notion of vagueness was prevalent, too.) The phrasing was rubato, tempos were constantly changing, meters were shifting, and rhythms were placed within this already vague atmosphere. Rhythmic vitality is not one aspect of Impressionism.

- Harmonies were also vague, but tonal. The rules of harmonic progressions were abandoned. Parallel chords of all sorts, including 7ths and 9ths were used to create color, not a tonal progression. Dissonances were common and were not prepared nor resolved. Whole tone and pentatonic scales were favored offering an oriental flare to this new Western style. Tonality took on an open-ended quality.

- All of the textures were employed and used for color and atmosphere.

- Traditional forms, such as variations and sonata form, were abandoned in favor of more simple, but often large-scale, binary and ternary forms.

- For the most part, Impressionistic music had a quiet, dream-like quality. When fortes were used, they were mostly short-lived.
- Because of the nature of Impressionism, new tone colors in the orchestration were created. Harps and flutes were two favored instruments and they were often paired together. Percussion instruments were used, but were never a focal point in this style.

II. Expressionism

- The more rebellious of the two styles, expressionism demonstrated a turning away from all expectations of traditional art music. Strong emotional expression was the goal. Melodies were optional. Harmonies could not be analyzed. Texture was indeterminable.
- What *did* remain traditional, at least in retrospect, were the elements of rhythm, form, and timbre. Binary and ternary forms were popular as were variations and even contrapuntal devices, all within an atonal system.
- Schoenberg and Berg employed a new type of "singing" called *Sprechstimme*. This was a sort of approximated-pitch speaking method.
- A new, organized compositional practice called 12-tone technique (or row) was utilized by Schoenberg. Each of the twelve pitches was taken once and ordered, then manipulated in a highly contrived manner into a musical composition. Interestingly, this highly organized method produced some of the most random *sounding* music of the Age.
- The most extraordinary advancement of Expressionism, by far, was the atonality that dominated its style. Through all of music's history, no matter the style, tonality of some sort was always the one common musical trait. Now it was abolished.

Other styles that emerged in the 20th century include:

- <u>Aleatoric</u> (Aleatory) music, or chance music, was a new concept of composition in which the composer left one or more musical elements in performance up to chance. Performances of this sort were never the same twice.

- <u>Electronische Musik</u> (electronic music) developed in Germany in the 1950s. The innovations in the field since then have been astounding. For modern music today, the fusion of technology (think mere electricity) and acoustic music has created an entirely different aesthetic from all those that have preceded us.

- <u>Minimalism</u> was a style of repetitive music that emerged in the 1960s and came to its artistic height in the 1980s. The style was based on the notion that small units of pitches, chords, or rhythms could be repeated with only slight variations over long periods of time.

- <u>Musique concrete</u> had far-reaching compositional effects on modern music. The French composer, Pierre Schaeffer (1910-1995) first developed this technique in the late 1940s. Musique concrete takes a recorded natural sound (a concrete sound) such as the dripping of water, the singing of birds, the passing of a train, or speaking voices, and then manipulates the sound by tape splicing it, mixing it and superimposing the sounds one on top of another. [I'm sure you are thinking about how our popular music has been effected by this innovation.]

- <u>Neo-classicism</u> was a return to the ideals of clarity and objectivity of the 18th century. This popular style from the 1910s and 20s utilized textures, topics, and forms from the past and combined them with modern harmony, tonality, and timbres.

- <u>Neo-romanticism</u> appealed to audiences who were waiting for music that they could understand and embrace. Dissonances were often more prevalent than they had been in the 19th century, but most romantic elements of melody, harmony, and texture were present. Neo-tonality, a non-functional tonality, was created for this new style.

- <u>Non-tonal</u> music was a style of composition that focused on musical elements other than pitch. Percussion ensembles benefited from this new style and were given a new status in modern art music.

- <u>Postmodernism</u> was an aesthetic attitude that developed in the late 1970s that focused on uniting all past elements of music (including those from the earlier parts of the 20th century) into a new eclectic style. This, up until now, has been the most inclusive style of music, expressing prejudices toward nothing. And, this style has crossed over into popular music of our day as artists have taken Gregorian chants and other historical pieces of music and have incorporated them into their songs in various ways.

Chapter 2

ℂℛ

An Chronological Overview of Composers and Personalities[1]

All of the composers are listed by their birthdates. If you do not know the year in which a composer was born, turn to page 148 to the alphabetical list.

Antiquity: ~ 500 B.C. to ~ 470s A.D.

(Sometimes presented as 300 B.C.E. - 400 C.E.)

⅄ We have about 45 complete pieces or fragments of ancient music ranging from 300 B.C. to 400 A.D.[2] All of these extant pieces use a system of ancient Greek musical notation. We know that the Romans were musically active too, but we don't have any of their surviving music.

Pythagoras:	(ca. 569 BC — ca. 475 BC), the Greek legendary founder of music theory; considered the first pure mathematician
Aeschylus:	(ca. 525 BC — 456 BC), Greek tragic poet, playwright, and musician
Euripides:	(ca. 485 BC — ca. 406 BC), Greek tragic poet, playwright, and musician; we believe that he was an advocate of the "New music" that exhibited coloratura skills and vivid emotion
Plato:	(ca. 429 BC — ca. 347 BC), influenced by Pythagoras; friend of Socrates; Greek; wrote *Republic* in 380 B.C.
Aristotle:	(ca. 384 BC — 322 BC), Greek father of Western intellectual thinking; wrote *Politics* in 330 B.C.
Aristoxenus:	(ca. 375-60 BC —?), Greek music theorist and pupil of Aristotle

---

1 The works listed under each composer are intended only to give the reader a general idea of the output of that composer. For detailed information, begin by looking at the work-list in the New Grove article for each composer. Additionally, composers marked with an "*" are studied in most Freshman-level courses and are considered essential to your knowledge.

2 The older delineation of "B.C." is often changed today to the more modern "B.C.E." Likewise, the "A.D." is now "C.E." This book will use the more traditional labels of B.C. and A.D.

Seikilos: (first century AD), composer and poet

Claudius Ptolemy: (ca. after 83 AD — 161), Greek mathematician, geographer, astronomer, and music theorist

Aristides Quintilianus: (fl. ca. 200 AD), author of the music treatise, *Peri mousikes* ("On music")

St. Ambrose: (ca. 340-397), Saint, bishop, politician; composer of hymns

St. Augustine: (354-430), music theorist; began a six-book treatise, *De Musica* ("On Music") in 387 AD

Middle Ages / Medieval Period: ~ 476 A.D. to 1420s

⅄ During the Middle Ages,[3] music was used extensively in the early church. There was also a flourishing popular-music culture of which we have significant examples. Melody is used primarily to convey words. Most composers were poets.

Anicius Manlius Severinus Boethius (ca. 480-ca. 524) music theorist   Roman writer and statesman; important as a
    with his *De institutione musica* ("The Fundmentals of Music", early 500s)

*Guido of Arezzo (ca. 991-after 1033) writings   Music theorist; he is credited with creating a system of precise pitch notation through lines and spaces on a staff; he advocated a method of sight-singing using the syllables, (*ut, re, mi, fa, sol, la*); his treatise, *Micrologus*, is the earliest and best treatise on musical composition of chant and polyphony

Wipo of Burgundy (ca. 995-ca. 1050)   Priest, poet, and composer (we believe)

---

[3]The reader will find a number of variations in the actual years that encompass each era. I suggest that we remain flexible in our thinking of these period dates, taking into consideration important issues of style.

William IX (1071-1127)
11 poems, 1 melody survives

Duke of Aquitaine, father of Eleanor; first of the noble troubadours

*Hildegard von Bingen (1098-1179)
77 melodies, morality play, books, poetry

Composer of the first morality play; known as the Sybil of the Rhine; writer, composer, theologian; her counsel was sought after by Kings and Popes

*Bernart de Ventadorn
(ca. 1130-40-ca. 1190-1200)
44 songs; we have 18 complete with melodies

Famous troubadour; perhaps the finest of the troubadour poets; very important musically

Giraut de Bornelh (ca. 1140-ca. 1200)
4 melodies survive including 1 alba; 77 poems total (most lost)

Troubadour; Dante ranks him second only to Arnaut Daniel

Raimbaud de Vacqueiras (1155-1207)
32 poems, 8 melodies survive

Troubadour; fluent in many languages

Richard the Lionheart (1157-99)
2 poems survive, only 1 with music

King of England from 1189-99; son of Eleanor of Aquitaine and Henry II; a trouvère; he never learned English

Gace Brulé (ca. 1160-after 1213)
69 poems, 57 melodies survive

One of the earliest trouvères and most famous of poets; melodies show influence of Gregorian Chant

*Léonin (fl. 1150s-ca. 1201)
Magnus Liber, collection of organum

(Magister Leoninus II); Master of organum purum at the Cathedral of Notre Dame, Paris; our information comes largely from Anonymous IV's writings

Arnaut Daniel (?1150-60-ca. 1200)
2 melodies survive; 18 poems

Dante esteemed him above all other troubadours; master of the "difficult" style; he took the poetic style to new heights

*Comtessa Beatriz de Dia (d. ca. 1212)
1 tenso, 4 cansos

Famous female troubadour; she has left us the only surviving melody by a female troubadour

*Walter von der Vogelweide
(ca. 1170-1230)

Poet and Minnesinger; worked at the Viennese court; he wrote the earliest surviving minnesinger melody

Aimeric de Peguilhan (ca. 1175-ca. 1230)
   54 poems, 6 melodies survive

Troubadour; his works were admired by many writers

Blondel de Nesle (ca. 1155/60-1200) trouvères;

One of the most important early his works show up in multiple manuscripts

*Pérotin [Perotinus] (fl. 1180-ca. 1238)
   organum, clausulae, conductus

Master of discant organum at the Cathedral of Notre Dame, Paris; supposed student of Leonin; wrote 3 and 4-voice organum

Peire Vidal (fl. ca. 1183-ca. 1205)
   40 poems, 13 melodies survive

Troubadour; eccentric character; wide ranging melodies

Neidhart von Reuental
   (ca. 1190-after 1236)
   ?57 poems, 17 melodies survive

Austrian Minnesinger; one of the earliest German poets; folk-like style; his works were the only Minnesinger songs printed in the Renaissance

Guillaume le Vinier (ca. 1190-1245)
   30 poems, most melodies survive

Trouvère and priest at Arras

Peire Cardenal (?1180-?1278)
   of 90 poems, 3 melodies survive

One of the most celebrated troubadours his time; satirical criticism of contemporary nobility and clergy

Thibaut IV (1201-53)
   63 melodies survive

Trouvère; Count of Champagne, King of Navarre (1234-53); he headed crusades to Jerusalem; prolific composer and poet

*Moniot d'Arras (fl. 1213-1239)
   23 poems, 13 melodies survive

Trouvère; wrote in several genres and forms; monk at Arras

Alfonso X ('El Sabio') (1221-84)

Spanish monarch; King of Castile and León; bother-in-law of Edward I of England; patron of literature and art; initiated the study of music at Salamanca University; helped compile "Cantigas de Santa María"

Guiraut Riquier (ca. 1230-ca. 1300)
   many melodies, some with
   religious texts

The last of the troubadours; lived in Spain under Alfonso X

*Adam de la Halle (ca. 1245-50-ca. 1285-8)
   chansons, musical plays,
   rondeaux, 7 motets

One of the last trouvères; wrote polyphony and studied in Paris

Anonymous IV (probably fl. 1250+)

Music theorist and his treatise of the same name, gives us information about Leonin and Perotin, and organum; we think he was a student from England

The Ars Nova in France: 1300–1350

⚐   The New style in France focused on new compositional techniques such as **isorhythm** and **hocket**. The most innovative accomplishments were in the area of rhythm.

*Philippe de Vitry (1291-1361)
     treatise: *Ars Nova*, 1322-23;
     motets
     bishop

Known as the "inventor of a new art," composer, poet, and theorist; established new tradition of mensural notation;

*Guillaume de Machaut (ca. 1300-77)
     important *Mass of Notre Dame*,
     23 motets, 19 lais, 42 ballades,
     33 virelais, 22 rondeaux

The leading composer and poet of the Ars Nova; his importance and innovations are extraordinary

Baude Cordier (fl. early 15th c.)

French composer; he wrote in the older style and in the new modern ars subtilior; his rondeau, *Belle bonne sage*, was published in musical notation in the shape of a heart.

The Trecento in Italy: 1300–1390s

Gherardello da Firenze
     (ca. 1320-25-1362 or 63)
     Mass sections, madrigals,
     ballate, caccia

Italian composer; ranks second in importance to Landini; priest

Jacopo da Bologna (fl. 1340-1386?)
     35 surviving pieces

Italian composer; virtuoso harpist; teacher of Landini; wrote a treatise on notation

*Francesco Landini (ca. 1325-97)
     155 works, mostly ballate

Known for his cadences; virtuoso organist; blind from early age; most celebrated musical personality of the Trecento; also an instrument maker

Moving Towards the Renaissance Style: 1390 – 1430s

Oswald von Wolkenstein (ca. 1376-1445)

Austrian poet and composer; used French notation; wrote polyphony; used German texts

*John Dunstaple (ca. 1390-1453)
    20 mass sections,
    2 complete masses,
    40 motets, 2 secular songs

The leading English composer; created a new consonant style of 3rds and 6ths that became the Renaissance style

Renaissance: 1430 to 1600

⋏ During the Renaissance, secular music became more popular and widespread. Polyphony was the primary texture in most genres. Melodies were numerous and simultaneous, and therefore often obscured. In the 1500s early versions of homophony emerged. Most composers wrote masses, motets, and after 1540, madrigals. The madrigal served as the vehicle for experimentation that helped lead into the Baroque style.

*Guillaume Dufay (ca. 1397-1474)
    8 Masses, 37 Mass sections,
    90 motets

Franco-Flemish; the first important Renaissance composer; used older medieval cadences

Gilles Binchois (ca. 1400-60)
    28 mass sections, 30 motets,
    4 Magnificats, 55 chansons

Early Renaissance composer; served at the Court of the Duke of Burgundy; Franco-Flemish

*Johannes Ockeghem (ca. 1410-97)
    10 masses, 9 motets,
    chansons

Bass singer; served 3 Kings; very respected; usually not much imitation; Franco-Flemish

Antoine Busnois (ca. 1430-1492)
    3 masses, 8 motets,
    63 chansons, 2 Magnificats

His chansons represent a transition to a new Renaissance secular polyphony

Johannes Tinctoris (ca. 1435- ca. 1511)   Franco-Flemish theorist, singer, and
    12 treatises, 4 masses,   composer
    2 motets, 7 chansons

Loyset Compère (ca. 1445-1518)   Franco-flemish composer, singer; worked
    2 masses, 4 mass sections,   in France and Italy; he was considered a
    3 motet cycles, 23 motets,   prominent contemporary of Josquin
    Magnificats, 49 chansons

Alexander Agricola (ca. 1446-1506)   Franco-Flemish; worked in France and
    8 masses, 25 motets, 100   Italy
    chansons (Italian and Dutch),
    carnival songs

*Josquin des Prez (ca. 1450-1521)   Considered by Martin Luther to be the
    18 masses, 100 motets,   "best of the composers of our time" and
    chansons   "the master of the notes"; he was said to
        have had no peer in music.

*Heinrich Isaac (ca. 1450-1517)   Italian who influenced German music;
    40 masses, 350 motets,   court composer to Maximilian I; served in
    German songs, frottole,   Florence as well
    100 cycles of the Proper

*Pierre de la Rue (ca. 1452-1518)   Leading composer at the Burgundian
    31 Masses, 37 motets,   court; never worked in Italy; very famous
    7 mass sections, Requiem,   in his day; frequent use of canon and
    37 chansons   ostinato

*Jacob Obrecht (ca. 1457-1505)   Made important contributions to large-
    26 masses, Marian antiphons,   scale forms and their unity
    32 motets, 30 secular works

Jean Mouton (before 1459-1522)   Worked in the French royal court;
    15 masses, 100 motets,   used canon exceptionally well
    20 chansons, Magnificats

Antoine Brumel (ca. 1460- 1512/13)   Franco-Flemish; worked in France and
    12 masses, 29 motets,   Italy; prominently published in his day
    3 Magnificats, chansons

Marco Cara (ca. 1465 – after 1525)   Italian composer and singer in Mantua;
    100 frottole   Isabella d'Este's favorite musician; raised
        the frottla to a level of sophistication

*Ottaviano Petrucci (1466-1539)   First music printer and publisher;
        preserved Renaissance music for us today

Bartolomeo Tromboncino
(ca. 1470- after 1534)
lamentations, 22 laude,
dramatic works, frottole

Italian composer at Mantua, Vicenza,
(where he murdered his wife and her
lover), Ferrara, and Florence

Philippe Verdelot (ca. 1480-85-?1530-32)

French; worked in Italian cities; famous
for his early madrigals which were often
homorhythmic in style

*Martin Luther (1483-1546)
German hymns, writings

German theologian and composer; he was
the founder of the Lutheran Church

Costanzo Festa (ca. 1485-90-1545)
4 masses, 40 motets,
30 hymns, 13 Magnificats,
madrigals

Italian composer; studied with Mouton
in Paris; worked in Rome; wrote litanies
for double chorus

Clément Janequin (ca. 1485-after 1558)
286 chansons

French; served the King of France;
master of the French chanson; wrote
famous programmatic chansons (battles,
birds, and chases)

Ludwig Senfl (ca. 1486-1542/3)
7 masses, motets, Magnificats,
250 German songs,
Lutheran chorale elaborations

Swiss German composer and singer;
Catholic, but admired Luther; master of
quodlibets

John Taverner (ca. 1490-1545)
8 masses, 25 motets

English; organist and choirmaster;
influenced by the Lutheran faith; wrote
for the Catholic liturgy

Claudin de Sermisy (ca. 1490-1562)
3 books of motets, masses,
Passion, 160 chansons

French composer and singer; widely
published in his day

*Adrian Willaert (ca. 1490-1562)
9 masses, 173 motets,
madrigals

Complex, continuous polyphony; strong
advocate of textual expression; studied
with Jean Mouton; served in Italian
courts; extraordinary teacher; worked in
Venice at St. Marks Cathedral

Hans Sachs (1494-1576)
stage productions, songs

German Meistersinger; wrote thousands
of songs (yes, thousands)

Pierre Attaingnant (1494-ca. 1551)

French music printer and publisher; used
movable type and a single impression

Nicolas Gombert (ca. 1495-ca. 1560)
 10 masses, 60 chansons,
 160 motets, 8 Magnificats

From Flanders; worked in Spanish court; master of counterpoint; leading figure between Josquin and Palestrina

Johann Walter (1496-1570)
 chorale settings, motets,
 Magnificats, Passions,
 instrumental canons

Protestant; German cantor and composer; collaborated with Luther to create music for the German reformed services

Christóbal Morales (ca. 1500-53)
 21 masses, 91 motets,
 16 Magnificats, 11 hymns

Spanish composer and singer; especially popular after his death

*Thomas Tallis (ca. 1505-85)
 30 motets (1 for 40 voices)
 3 masses, Psalms, anthems,
 Lamentations

English organist; taught Byrd; he was Catholic during Henry VIII's troubled years; wrote both for the Latin and the reformed English liturgies

*Jacques Arcadelt (ca. 1507-ca. 1568)
 volumes of madrigals,
 chansons, masses

Dutch; worked in Rome and Paris; famous for his early madrigals and his 3 to 7-voice masses (often homorhythmic style); well published in the 16th c.

Tilman Susato (ca. 1510-15-1570 or later)
 many dance arrangements

German printer, publisher, and composer

Jacobus Clemens (ca. 1510- ca. 1556)
 15 masses, 230 motets,
 89 chansons, 2 Magnificats,
 2 mass fragments, 159 Dutch
 polyphonic Psalms

Also known as Clemens non Papa (indicating, "not the Pope"); worked in Spain for Charles V

Nicola Vicentino (1511-ca. 1576)
 2 books of madrigals, motets

Advocated half steps (chromatic) and quarter-tones (microtonal); theorist and composer; built a harpsichord with 36 keys per octave; innovator in tuning systems

*Cipriano de Rore (1515/16-65)
 125 madrigals, 65 motets,
 3 masses, 8 Psalms,
 Magnificats, 1 Passion

Flemish; worked in Ferrara and Parma; associated with Willaert

Gioseffo Zarlino (1517-90)

Important Italian theorist of counterpoint; composer; wrote *Le istitutioni harmoniche* in 1558 which helped establish the field of counterpoint

Vincenzo Galilei (ca. 1520-91)

Italian composer, theorist, lutenist; father of Galileo Galilei, the astronomer; studied with Zarlino; champion of Greek music and member of the Florentine Camerata

Giovanni Animuccia (ca. 1520-1571)
    1 book of masses, Magnificats,
    4 books of madrigals, laude

Palestrina's predecessor in Rome; helped to establish the Roman style

Adrien le Roy (ca. 1520-98)
    chansons, lute pieces,
    accompanied songs

French publisher, printer, composer, lutenist, author; ran the firm LeRoy and Ballard; author of pedagogical books for plucked strings

*Philipp de Monte (1521-1603)
    1073 secular madrigals, 38 masses,
    319 motets, 144 sacred madrigals,
    45 chansons

At the Viennese and Prague courts; religious; Franco-Flemish; mixed polyphony and homophony; one of the most prolific composers of the Renaissance

*Giovanni P. da Palestrina
    (1525/26-1594)
    104 masses, 375 motets,
    madrigals (sacred and secular)

Became an icon of Renaissance music for future generations; Roman style; responded to the requests of the Council of Trent to reform Catholic church music; mostly contrapuntal liturgical music

Costanzo Porta (1528/9-1601)
    3 books of madrigals,
    1 book of Masses, 4 books
    of motets, keyboard works

Pupil of Willaert; teacher of Viadana; tried to please the Council of Trent

Claude Le Jeune (1528/30-1600)
    11 motets, chansons,
    vernacular Psalms

Parisian intellectual; respected by Kings; dedicated to the reform of music and poetry "musique mesuree a l'antique"; wrote Huguenot psalms

Francisco Guerrero (1528-99)
    17 masses, 2 Requiems,
    4 books of motets, Passions,
    Magnificats, music for Vespers,
    Spanish spiritual madrigals

Spanish composer; worked in Spain; student of Morales

Anthoine [Antoine] de Bertrand
    (1530-40-ca. 1580)
    chansons, sacred songs,
    hymns, Latin motets

French composer; used much chromaticism and some microtones!; published 3 books of secular polyphony

*Orlando di Lasso (1532-94)
    60 masses, 530 motets,
    150 chansons, 175 Italian
    madrigals, 90 German Lieder,
    100 Magnificats

Also Roland de Lassus; widely traveled; employed G. Gabrieli in 1575; over 2000 compositions in all languages

*Andrea Gabrieli (1532/35-1585)
    masses, motets, Psalms,
    vocal concerti, madrigals,
    keyboard and instrumental works

Italian organist, composer, teacher; uncle of Giovanni; worked in Venice; pupil of Willaert; innovative orchestration

Lodovico Agostini (1534-90)
    9 volumes of madrigals,
    sacred music

Italian composer; worked at the Vatican and Ferrara

*Count Giovanni Bardi (1534-1612)
    Intermedi, a treatise

Leader of the Florentine Camerata in the late 1570s-90s

Alessandro Striggio (ca. 1536/37-1592)
    2 masses, motets,
    Intermedii

Italian lutenist and composer at Florentine Court; wrote one motet for 40 voices which was performed by instruments

*Giaches de Wert (1535-96)
    15 volumes of madrigals,
    motets, hymns

Pupil of de Rore; served the Dukes of Manuta and Parma; stormy personal life; text declamation important to him; influenced Monteverdi; friend of the poet, Tasso; wrote madrigals for the Concerto della donne[4]

Marc Antonio Ingegneri (ca. 1535-1592)
    6 books of madrigals, much
    sacred music

Italian composer who helped establish the Roman style

Battista Giovanni Guarini (1538-1612)

Italian poet and dramatist; his poetry was set by many Baroque composers; he created the pastoral vogue that lasted into the 18th century

*William Byrd (ca. 1540-1623)
    3 masses, 175 motets,
    anthems

English; Catholic composer writing both Protestant and Catholic music in England; greatest English composer of his time

---

4 The *Concerto della donne* (ensemble of women) was a group of virtuosic singers employed at Ferrara in the 1580s. The women included Laura Peverara, Anna Guarini, Livia d'Arco, Tarquinia Molza, Leonora Sanvitale, among others.

Giovanni Maria Nanino (1543/44-1607)
    madrigals, canzonets,
    church music, canons

Italian composer who helped carry on the tradition of Palestrina's Roman style; pupil of Palestrina; in 1580 started a music school with his brother

Torquato Tasso (1544-95)

Italian poet; his works have been favored by composers for centuries

Luzzasco Luzzaschi (ca. 1545-1607)
    7 books of madrigals,
    instrumental pieces

Pupil of de Rore; served at Ferrara; Frescobaldi's teacher; wrote 8 books of madrigals, one with written-out keyboard accompaniment; wrote madrigals for the Concerto delle donne

Jacques Salmon (ca. 1545-86?)

French composer and singer; one of the composers credited with writing the first ballet, *Ballet comique de la Reine* in 1581 with composer, Beaulieu

*Tomás Luis de Victoria (1548-1611)
    20 masses, 50 motets,
    Magnificats, hymns

Spanish; continued Palestrina's Roman style in Spain; studied in Rome; sacred-music composer; the greatest Spanish composer in the Renaissance

Orazio Vecchi (1550-1605)
    dramatic works, sacred and
    secular vocal works

Italian composer; he is remembered as a pioneer of dramatic music in the 16th century

*Luca Marenzio (1553/54-1599)

    9 books of madrigals, 75 sacred motets

The leading madrigal composer of the late 16th century; worked in Rome, Ferrara, Florence, and Warsaw (serving the King of Poland); influenced the English madrigal

Giovanni Giacomo Gastoldi
    (ca. 1554-1609)
    madrigals, sacred vocal
    works, instrumental pieces

Famous for his 2 sets of balletti (strophic vocal dance-songs with passages of nonsense syllables); influenced the English

*Thomas Morley (1557/58-1602)
    edited the "Triumphs of
    Oriana" (1601)

English; contributed to the development of the English madrigal; important in music publication and printing; probably a pupil of Byrd; wrote in 1597, *A Plaine and Easie Introduction to Practicall Musicke* [sic]

Giovanni Bernardino Nanino
(ca. 1560-1623)
motets and madrigals

Italian composer and teacher who helped carry on the Roman style of Palestrina; one of the first Roman composers to use basso continuo; brother of Giovanni Maria

*Carlo Gesualdo (ca. 1561-1613)
6 books of madrigals,
2 books of motets,
1 book of responsories,
keyboard works

Known for his chromaticism,; Neapolitan Prince of Venosa; murdered his wife and lover in 1590; leading composer of madrigals; extreme expressive intensity; Stravinisky was fascinated with his music; friends with the poet Tasso

Jan Pieterszoon Sweelinck (1562-1621)
33 chansons, 19 madrigals,
153 Psalm settings, 70 keyboard works

Organist in Amsterdam; teacher; helped to lay the foundations of German organ music

*Claudio Monteverdi (1567-1643)
(see Early Baroque)

Ahead of his time; took music into a new style (*secunda prattica* vs. the older, *prima prattica*)

John Farmer (ca. 1570-fl. 1591-1601)
madrigals, instrumental works,
4-part Psalm settings

English composer and organist

*Thomas Weelkes (1576-1623)
madrigals and anthems

English organist; drinking problem

Lambert de Beaulieu (fl. ca. 1576-90)

French composer and singer; one of the composers credited with writing the first ballet, *Ballet comique de la Reine* in 1581 with Salmon

---

<u>Famous Italian Courts in the Renaissance and Early Baroque</u>

Florence:	de'Medici family
Milan:	Sforza family
Ferrara:	d'Este dukes
Mantua:	Gonzaga family

Baroque: 1600–1730s /1750

⅄ The Baroque is typically divided into three parts: early, mid, and late (or high). Around the turn of the 17th century opera was born and basso continuo became a staple in music composition and performance. Some of the most modern innovations of music took place during these 130 years.

The Early Baroque: 1600–~1650

Emilio de'Cavalieri (ca. 1550-1602) composed the first surviving play set entirely to music, *Rappresentatione di Anima. . . cantando* (Rome, 1600)

Roman nobleman; one of the founders of opera; the first to publish a figured bass; also an organist, singing teacher, dancer, choreographer

*Giulio Caccini (1551-1618)
4 stage works, more than 75 songs or arias

One of the founders of opera; gave a description of the new singing style in his book of "songs" of 1602, *Le nuove musiche*

*Giovanni Gabrieli (ca. 1557-1612)
90 motets, grand concertos

Noted for his use of instruments in his sacred music; nephew of Andrea

Lodovico Grossi Viadana (ca. 1560-1627)
22 volumes of motets,
4 books of madrigals,
1 instrumental sinfonie

Wrote the earliest known example of liturgical monody (1607); was the first to compose and publish a continuo part for a collection of sacred vocal concerti (1602); wrote in the *stile moderno* (modern style)

Hieronymus Praetorius (1560-1629)
100 motets (some up to 20 parts)

German organist and composer; (not related to Michael); used the Venetian polychoral style; wrote Latin and German sacred songs

*Jacopo Peri (1561-1633)
20 stage works, 30 songs

Another founder of opera; claimed to be the first in 1597 with his *Dafne*

Jacopo Corsi (1561-1602)

Patron and composer; member of the Florentine Camerata; contributed to Peri's first opera *Dafne* of 1597; in 1600 he sponsored the premiere of Peri's *Euridice* and played harpsichord in the performance

Ottavio Rinuccini (1562-1621)

Italian librettist and poet; important librettist that worked with Monteverdi, among others

John Bull (ca. 1562-1628)
 27 keyboard works, songs, sacred music, 120 canons

English composer and organist; virtuoso virginalist

*John Dowland (ca. 1563-1626)
 3 books of songs, many pieces for lute, some sacred music

English, possibly Irish; lutenist and the leading composer of lute music; Catholic; served in the court of Denmark; late in life appointed in London as one of the King's lutes

Hans Leo Hassler (1564-1612)
 Latin Masses and motets, German songs, Italian madrigals, instrumental works for both ensembles and keyboards

North German Lutheran composer and organist; studied with A. Gabrieli; poly-choral style

*William Shakespeare (1564-1616)

English playwright and poet; he has been an important force in the field of music from his day to ours

*Claudio Monteverdi (1567-1643)
 8 books of Madrigals, Vespers, 13 operas, not all survived

The most important composer of the early Baroque; one of the inventors of the new *seconda prattica* (second practice-or modern style)

Thomas Campion (1567-1620)
 Masques, 5 volumes of ayres (Airs)

English poet and composer; he experimented by imitating the Florentine monodists

Adriano Banchieri (1568-1634)
 Treatises on organ playing and continuo practice, madrigal comedies, 20 volumes of sacred music, 20 books of secular music

Italian composer, theorist, organist; wrote under various pseudonyms

*Florentine Camerata
 (1570s-90s)

Beginning in the 1570s, a group of intellectuals that met to discuss the arts—members included Caccini, Peri, Girolamo Mei, Vincenzo Galilei

Salamone Rossi (ca. 1570-ca. 1630)
 4 books of sonatas and

Italian composer of Jewish descent; violinist; worked in Mantua; among the

dances for string ensemble, madrigals, dramatic music, Jewish Psalms

earliest composers to use trio sonata texture (1607-08)

Michael Praetorius (ca. 1571-1621)
Lutheran chorale motets

North-German composer and organist; helped to lay the foundations of German organ music

Agostino Agazzari (1578-1640)
dramatic works, 5 books of madrigals, sacred vocal works, writings

Italian composer and organist; wrote an important treatise on thoroughbass (figured bass)

Marco da Gagliano (1582-1643)
15 dramatic works, madrigals, sacred Italian and Latin vocal works

Italian composer; he was one of the most important Italian musicians in the early Baroque

Sigismondo d'India (ca. 1582-1629)
songs, duets, madrigals, sacred works, 3 stage works

Italian composer and singer; besides Monteverdi, d'India was the most distinguished Italian composer of secular vocal works in the early Baroque

*Orlando Gibbons (1583-1625)
sacred choral music, anthems, consort music

English; composer of Anglican Church anthems

*Girolamo Frescobaldi (1583-1643)
instrumental works, sacred and secular vocal works

First modern keyboard virtuoso and composer; he was the most influential keyboard composer of the early Baroque

Giulio Strozzi (1583-1652)

Italian dramatist, librettist, and poet; father of Barbara Strozzi; his opera librettos were set to music from the 1620s on

Alessandro Grandi (1586-1630)
madrigals, motets, cantatas, songs with basso continuo

North Italian composer; very important in his time; wrote church music in the new concertato style

Johann Hermann Schein (1586-1630)

German composer and poet; worked at the Leipzig Thomaskirche before Bach; was influenced by the Italian madrigal and monody when writing his Lutheran church music

Samuel Scheidt (1587-1654)
150+ German choral works,
Latin choral music, chorales,
instrumental works, canons

German composer and organist; he
combined counterpoint with the new
Italian concerto style

Francesca Caccini (1587-1641)
9 dramatic works, songs

Daughter of Giulio; the first composer to
have her Italian opera staged outside of
Italy; virtuoso singer and teacher

Tarquinio Merula (ca. 1594-1665)
opera, sacred and secular vocal
works, instrumental works

Italian composer, violinist, and organist;
among the first to compose motets with
instrumental string accompaniment
(1624);
worked in Warsaw and Italy

Francesco Manelli (1594-1667)
11 dramatic works (all the music
is lost), other vocal works

Italian composer, singer, impresario, and
poet; he helped establish the public
operatic tradition in Venice with librettist
Benedetto Ferrari

Heinrich Scheidemann (ca. 1595-1663)
17 chorales, 12 preludes

German composer, teacher, and organist;
a leading composer of organ music

Luigi Rossi (1597/98-1653)
operas, oratorios, cantatas

A leading composer of Roman cantatas;
singing teacher, lutenist, and keyboardist

Marco Marazzoli (ca. 1602/08-1662)
cantatas, oratorios, comic
operas

Italian composer, singer, and harpist; he
was a leading composer in his day; he was
one of the first to compose comic operas

Benedetto Ferrari (1603/4-1681)
operas, librettos, ballets, vocal
chamber works, writings

Italian composer, poet, librettist, and
impresario; he established the tradition of
public operatic performances in Venice
with the help of Francesco Manelli

*Giacomo Carissimi (1605-74)
3 masses, 100 motets, 15
oratorios, 150+ cantatas

A leading composer of Roman
cantatas and oratorios; teacher of
Charpentier

Johann Jakob Froberger (1616-67)
keyboard and vocal works

German composer and keyboardist; pupil
of Frescobaldi; synthesized French,
Italian, and German styles of keyboard
music

The Middle Baroque: 1650–1700

*Heinrich Schütz (1585-1672)
   madrigals, hundreds   of choral
   works

Most important German composer of the
Middle Baroque; studied in Venice

Francesco Cavalli (1602-76)
   at least 34 operas, cantatas,
   arias, sacred vocal works

Italian composer, singer, teacher, and
organist; he was the leading composer in
Venice after Monteverdi; extraordinarily
famous during his day

Henri Du Mont (ca. 1610-84)
   grand motets, motets, arias,
   psalms

French composer and keyboardist

Andreas Hammerschmidt (1611-75)
   400+ sacred vocal works
   (motets, concertos, arias),
   instrumental works

German composer and organist;
composed independent instrumental
ensemble music (unusual for the time)

*Barbara Strozzi (1619-77)
   madrigals, cantatas, arias

Virtuoso singer and most prolific
composer of cantatas in the 17th century

Isabella Leonarda (1620-1704)
   sacred motets, masses

A nun who, at age 73, published several
new Baroque instrumental genres (solo
and trio sonatas)

Matthew Locke (ca. 1621-77)
   anthems, motets, consort pieces,
   keyboard works, songs

English composer of chamber and
dramatic music; he was very prolific

Antonio Cesti (1623-69)
   15 stage works, cantatas

Outstanding composer of operas and
secular cantatas

Giovanni Andrea Bontempi
   (ca. 1624-1705)
   4 operas, other vocal works,

Italian composer, singer, author,
historian, and architect; he wrote
the first history of music in Italian
writings (*Historia musica*, 1695)

*Giovanni Legrenzi (1626-90)
   19 operas, 7 oratorios, sacred
   and secular vocal works,
   instrumental works

Italian composer and organist

*Jean-Baptiste Lully (1632-87)
   16 operas, 30+ ballets, motets,
   instrumental works

Establisher of French opera and ballet;
dancer and violinist

*Dieterich Buxtehude (ca. 1637-1707)
    100+ sacred vocal works, 100+
    works for organ, instrumental
    works

German organist and composer; most
important organ composer before J. S.
Bach, and respected by him

Alessandro Stradella (1639-82)
    33 stage works, masses, motets,
    cantatas, arias, oratorios

Italian composer; prolific and important
in his day

Johann Christoph Bach (1642-1703)
    arias, motets, vocal concertos,
    instrumental works

German composer and organist; most
important Bach family member before
J. S. Bach

*Marc-Antoine Charpentier (1643-1704)
    11 masses, magnificats, motets,
    antiphons, psalms, oratorios,
    airs, cantatas, operas, incidental
    music, instrumental works

Composer of French opera; pupil of
Carissimi; equal to Lully and extremely
prolific

*John Blow (1648/49-1708)

English composer of odes; teacher of
Purcell

*Arcangelo Corelli (1653-1713)
    6 published collections

Most important Italian composer of
sonatas and concertos; also the most
influential violinist of the Baroque

*Johann Pachelbel (1653-1706)
    liturgical organ music, Protestant
    church music, other keyboard
    works, 2 masses

German composer and organist

Agostino Steffani (1654-1728)
    Chamber duets for 2 sopranos
    and basso continuo

Italian composer and diplomat; his
chamber duets are an important stage of
Italian vocal music before Handel

Michel-Richard de Lalande (1657-1726)
    leading composer of grand
    motets, airs, instrumental
    works, ballets, operas

French composer and keyboardist; Louis
XIV's favorite composer

*Giuseppe Torelli (1658-1709)

Contributed the most to the development
of the concerto around 1700.

*Henry Purcell (1659-95)
    songs, anthems, sacred music,
    6 stage works, incidental music,
    keyboard works

Most important English composer in the
17th century

The Late Baroque: 1700–1730s /1750

*Alessandro Scarlatti (1660-1725)
    69 operas, serenatas, oratorios,
    arias, hundreds of cantatas,
    10 masses, motets, madrigals,
    keyboard works, concertos,
    theoretical and pedagogical works

Important Italian composer; teacher in Naples; his death ends Baroque opera

Johann Joseph Fux (1660-1741)
    operas, vocal works, a few
    church sonatas, writings

Austrian composer and theorist; continued the church-music tradition and used Palestrina's style as a teaching tool; his counterpoint textbook from 1725 was used by most musicians in the 18th century (*Gradus ad Parnassum*)

Johann Kuhnau (1660-1722)
    Latin and German choral music,
    keyboard works, writings

German composer, keyboardist, theorist, scholar, writer, and lawyer; he left us some early examples of interesting program music

Elisabeth-Claude Jacquet de la Guerre
    (1665-1729)
    ballets, operas, chamber music,
    3 volumes of cantatas

She was called "the marvel of our century"; educated in Louis XIV's court; lived in Paris; renowned harpsichordist

*François Couperin (1668-1733)
    sacred and secular vocal works,
    chamber music, 27 ordres (sets)
    of keyboard works

French composer, keyboardist; one of the most important French composers

Antonio Caldara (ca. 1670-1736)
    90 stage works, oratorios, vocal
    works, a few sonatas

Italian composer; he was one of the most prolific composers in his day

Tomaso Giovanni Albinoni (1671-1750/51)
    about 81 stage works, 100 sonatas,
    50 solo cantatas, 59 concertos

Italian composer who wrote operas and instrumental music; he was very popular in his day; Bach knew his works

Reinhard Keiser (1674-1739)
    at least 80 operas, cantatas,
    sacred vocal works, serenatas

German composer; he was the central figure in German opera in the Late Baroque

*Antonio Vivaldi (1678-1741)
 425 concerti grossi, 350 solo
 concerti, 60 ripieni concerti,
 45 double concerti, sonatas,
 masses, psalms, motets, cantatas,
 oratorios, 45 operas, serenatas

Italian composer; he laid the foundations for late Baroque instrumental music; teacher; pioneer of orchestral music; but, virtually forgotten by his contemporaries at his death

*Georg Philipp Telemann (1681-1767)
 cantatas, Passions, oratorios,
 masses, psalms, motets, operas,
 overtures, concertos, sonatas,
 quartets and quintets, keyboard
 works, theoretical publications

The most prolific German composer of his day; more popular than J. S. Bach during the Baroque

*Jean-Philippe Rameau (1683-1764)
 30+ dramatic works, cantatas,
 arias, keyboard works, other
 instrumental works, theoretical
 publications

French composer and theorist

Francesco Durante (1684-1755)
 sacred dramas, masses, motets,
 psalms, Magnificats, antiphons,
 cantatas, duets, concertos,
 sonatas, fugues, pedagogical
 works

Galant Italian composer and teacher; a leading composer of church music; Neapolitan

John Gay (1685-1732)
 plays and poems

An English playwright and poet who innovated a new genre, the Ballad opera, when he wrote *The Beggar's Opera* in 1728 as a satire on politics and partly on Handel's opera seria.

*Johann Sebastian Bach (1685-1750)
 205+ cantatas (mostly Lutheran),
 Mass, Magnificat, motets, suites,
 oratorios, Passions, fugues,
 concertos, sonatas, keyboard
 works, chorales

Considered the Baroque master; wrote no operas; master of counterpoint; he became an icon to us today

*Georg Friedrich Händel (1685-1759)
 46 dramatic works, oratorios,
 odes, Latin and English church
 music, Italian cantatas, duets and
 trios with basso continuo, songs,
 concertos, suites, overtures,
 sonatas, keyboard works

German musician; lived in England, inventor of the English oratorio; Beethoven respected him above all others

*Domenico Scarlatti (1685-1757)
  Sonatas for harpsichord; some
  vocal works

Son of Alessandro; keyboard composer
and virtuoso; lived in Spain and Portugal

Nicola Porpora (1686-1768)
  50 dramatic works, cantatas,
  oratorios, sacred operas,
  chamber and orchestral works

Italian composer and singing teacher

Francesco Geminiani (1687-1762)
  sonatas, concertos, symphonies,
  7 treatises

Italian composer, violinist, teacher, and
theorist; he was one of the greatest violin
virtuosos of his day

Giuseppe Tartini (1692-1770)
  vocal works, violin concertos,
  other concertos, chamber music,
  writings

Galant Italian composer, violinist,
teacher, and theorist; extremely
important as a violin teacher and as an
assimilator of the galant and
empfindsam styles

Leonardo Vinci (ca. 1696-1730)
  11 Neapolitan comedies, 24
  serious operas, a few other
  vocal and instrumental works

Galant Italian composer; leader (for a
time) of the new style of Italian opera

*Johann Joachim Quantz (1697-1773)
  204 sonatas, 300+ concertos,
  duets, capriccios, vocal works,
  published treatise *On Playing
  the Flute*, 1752

German composer; flutist and flute
teacher for Fredrick the Great in Berlin

Francesco Antonio Vallotti (1697-1780)
  masses, choral and vocal sacred
  music, writings

Italian composer and theorist; he was
important in the field of church music

Johann Gottlieb Graun (1702/3-71)
  sonatas, sinfonias, trio, concertos

German composer and a creator of
instrumental music of the classic era;
brother of Carl Heinrich

Carl Heinrich Graun (1703/04-59)
  36 Italian operas, sacred and
  secular vocal works, 40 concertos,
  chamber music

German composer; helped to preserve
Italian opera in Germany

Giovanni Battista Martini (Padre)
(1706-84)
about 1500 compositions, of which
1000 are canons, writings

Italian teacher, composer, and writer;
he was the leading teacher in the 18th
century; his surviving letters are
important to music history

*Giovanni Battista Pergolesi (1710-36)
10+ dramatic works, sacred vocal
works, arias, chamber cantatas,
instrumental works

Galant Neapolitan composer; he
died young and his achievements were
romanticized after his death; his
intermezzo, *La serva padrona* sparked
the war of the bouffons in Paris in 1752.

The Classic Period: 1740s-1810s

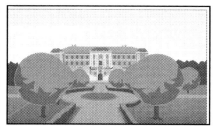

A The Classic period previously has been assigned a
variety of dates including, 1775-1825, 1725-1800,
1750-1800, and so on. Truly, the new classic style
was emerging in the new Italian operas of the
1720s and 30s. At the other end of the period
there were some composers who were pushing
out of classicism into Romanticism by the 1810s,
while other composers continued the basic traits
of the classic era into the 1820s.

Classic: 1740s – 1810s

*Pietro Metastasio (1698-1782)
27 three-act heroic operas,
several other dramatic works,
8 oratorios, serenatas, poems

Court poet in Vienna; most important
author of librettos for the 18th c.; his
libretti were set over 800 times in the 18th
and 19th centuries.

Johann Adolf Hasse (1699-1783)
63 operas, intermezzi, cantatas,
oratorios, masses, Requiems,
motets, much other vocal and
choral music, arias, concertos,
quartets, sonatas, other keyboard
works

German composer of Italian opera; from
the 1730s to the 1760s he was the most
admired composer of opera seria in Italy
and Germany; he was praised by most

*Giovanni Battista Sammartini
(1700/01-1775)
symphonies, concertos, overtures,
quartets, sonatas, 5 stage works,
sacred and secular vocal works

Galant Italian composer and inventor of
the symphony in Milan, 1730s+

*Farinelli (Carlo Broschi) (1705-82)

One of the most famous castrati in the 18th c.; trained by Porpora

Baldassare Galuppi (1706-85)
    over 100 operas, cantatas,
    oratorios, sonatas, 125 other
    instrumental works

Galant Italian composer, instrumentalist; key in the development of 18th-century comic opera; Burney considered him the best composer of comic opera in Italy

Carlo Goldoni (1707-93)
    55 opera buffa, 7 serious operas,
    intermezzi, writings

Italian playwright and librettist; responsible for elevating opera buffa to an art form

*Franz Xaver Richter (1709-89)
    symphonies, concertos, sonatas,
    string quartets, oratorios,
    masses, cantatas, motets

German composer, teacher, and singer; the real inventor of the string quartet; one of the foremost Mannheim composers

Franz Benda (1709-86)
    17 symphonies, chamber music,
    a few songs

Bohemian violinist, teacher, and composer; Charles Burney greatly praised him; brother of Johann Georg Benda

Caffarelli (Gaetano Majorani) (1710-83)

Famous castrato in the 18th c.; also trained by Porpora, who preferred Caffarelli to Farinelli

Wilhelm Friedemann Bach (1710-84)
    keyboard works, concertos,
    chamber music, sinfonias,
    cantatas, writing

German composer; son of J. S. Bach; known as the "Halle Bach" for his work in that town; gifted, but troubled

Domenico Alberti (ca. 1710-40)
    dramatic works, sonatas

Galant Italian composer, singer, and harpsichordist; known for his galant style and his simple, broken-chord accompaniment (now called Alberti bass)

Georg Anton Benda (1722-95)
    Singspiels, opera seria, cantatas,
    melodramas, symphonies,

    chamber music, other vocal works

Bohemian composer; important during his day as a composer of church music and stage music; brother of Franz Benda

*Prince Nikolaus J. Eszterházy (1714-90)

Haydn's patron and employer until 1790

Niccolò Jommelli (1714-74)
  64 serious operas, 21 comic operas, serenatas, pasticcios, oratorios, Passions, cantatas, masses, liturgical vocal works, sonatas, concertos, quartets

Galant Italian composer; important to opera reforms in the middle of the century; considered one of the greatest composers of his day; respected by Mozart

*Carl Philipp Emanuel Bach (1714-88)
  19 symphonies, keyboard works, hundreds of sonatas, concertos, arias, songs, choral music, theoretical works

Galant; Eldest son of J. S. Bach; wrote in both Baroque and classic styles; associated with *Empfindsamkeit* (*Empfindsam* style, or the "sentimental" style); worked for 30 years in Berlin for Frederick the Great

*Christoph Willibald Gluck (1714-87)
  operas, ballets, some vocal works, a few sonatas

German opera-reform composer, often considered Baroque; created a new balance between music and drama; jealous of Mozart

Georg Christoph Wagenseil (1715-77)
  13 operas, masses, oratorios, symphonies, concertos, chamber music, writings

Austrian composer, teacher, and keyboardist; he wrote in Baroque and galant styles

*Johann Stamitz (1717-57)
  58 symphonies, concertos, chamber music. orchestral trios, sacred vocal works

Galant, symphonic innovator in Mannheim; conductor, violinist, and teacher; he helped to establish the symphonic genre

Leopold Mozart (1719-87)
  vocal and choral music, chamber music, symphonies, keyboard works, concertos, writings

Composer, violinist, teacher, theorist, and father of Wolfgang

Carl Friedrich Abel (1723-87)
  symphonies, overtures, concertos, chamber music, music for viola da gamba

German composer and viola da gamba player; he and J. C. Bach set up a famous concert series in London

Giovanni Marco Rutini (1723-97)
  operas, oratorios, cantatas, harpsichord sonatas, a few piano works

Italian composer, teacher, and keyboardist; his keyboard works represent a transition from works for harpsichord to works for piano

*Dr. Charles Burney (1726-1814)
  histories and memoirs

Music historian, author, and organist who traveled Europe and wrote about his observations

Tommaso Traetta (1727-79)
    44 operas, arias, vocal works,
    choral music, a few instrumental
    works

Italian composer and teacher; important as an opera reform composer in the middle of the 18th century

Niccolò Piccinni (1728-1800)
    at least 110 operas, oratorios,
    other vocal works, a few
    chamber works

Italian composer; he was a central figure in Italian and French opera from 1750 to 1800; admired by Burney as one of the four greatest composers in Italy with Sacchini, Jommelli, and Galuppi

Johann Adam Hiller (1728-1804)
    14 Singspiels, choral music,
    editions, writings

German composer and writer

Anton Cajetan Adlgasser (1729-77)
    oratorios, masses, other vocal
    works, 1 opera, a few symphonies,
    writings

German composer and organist; a transitional figure in German music from the Baroque style to the classic style; Mozart praised his counterpoint

Antonio Sacchini (1730-86)
    45 operas, oratorios, masses,
    2 symphonies, chamber music

Italian composer; admired by Burney as one of the four greatest composers in Italy along with Jommelli, Galuppi, and Piccinni; his serious operas were most respected

Christian Cannabich (1731-98)
    ballets, symphonies, concertos,
    string quartets, chamber music

Conductor, composer, and violinist in Mannheim; one of the foremost Mannheim composers

*Franz Joseph Haydn (1732-1809)
    106 symphonies, 83 string
    quartets, 20 operas, choral music,
    chamber music, piano works

The primary German composer who served as inventor and mover to the new classic style; teacher, keyboardist, and violinist

Pierre-Augustin Beaumarchais (1732-99)

French writer; remembered in music for his trilogy, which included *The Barber of Seville* (1772) and *The Marriage of Figaro* (1781)

François-Joseph Gossec (1734-1829)
    23 stage works, symphonies,
    chamber music, revolutionary
    vocal music

Netherlands composer active in France; he was central to Parisian musical life and contributed to the development of French music

*Johann Christian Bach (1735-82)
    Symphonies, operas, church
    music, keyboard works, concertos

Worked in Milan and London; son of J. S. Bach; friend and influence to Mozart; set up concert series in London with Abel

Johann Georg Albrechtsberger
    (1736-1809): keyboard works,
    oratorios, cantatas, symphonies,
    string quartets, writings

Austrian composer, teacher, organist, and theorist; he is remembered mostly for his contrapuntal works

Michael Haydn (1737-1806)
    symphonies, masses, operas,
    cantatas, divertimentos, dances,
    choral music, chamber music

Brother of Franz Joseph; worked in Salzburg; contributed to 18th choral music

Johann Baptist Vanhal (1739-1813)
    73 symphonies, concertos,
    much chamber music,
    instrumental works, writings

Czech composer and teacher; active mostly in Vienna; important to instrumental music

Anna Amalia, Duchess of Saxe-Weimar
    (1739-1807)
    2 German Singspiels, chamber
    music, songs, an oratorio, a few
    choral works

Niece of Frederick the Great; made Weimar into an important musical center

Carl Ditters von Dittersdorf (1739-99)
    symphonies, Singspiels, opera
    buffa, masses, symphonies,
    concertos, chamber music

Austrian composer and violinist; part of the Viennese school; fluent in many genres

Christian Friedrich Daniel Schubart
    (1739-91)
    songs, keyboard works

German composer, poet, keyboardist, and writer; Burney praised his keyboard playing for its virtuosity

Giovanni Paisiello (1740-1816)
    91 operas, cantatas, oratorios,
    masses, other vocal works,
    concertos, quartets, sonatas,
    pedagogical works

Italian composer and teacher; he was one of the most successful and prolific opera composers of the late 18th century

André-Ernest-Modeste Grétry
    (1741-1813)
    opera comique, serious operas,
    ballets, chamber music, vocal
    works, revolutionary songs

French composer; contributed especially to the development of French opera

*Luigi Boccherini (1743-1805)
    91 string quartets, 90+ string
    quintets, sonatas, sextets, octets,
    symphonies, choral music, arias

Italian composer and cellist; prolific

Marianne Martínez (1744-1812)
    oratorios, 4 masses, cantatas,
    2 keyboard concertos, choral
    music, an overture, 2 piano sonatas

Austrian composer of Spanish descent;
studied with Metastasio, Porpora, and
Haydn; singer and keyboard player;
wrote works also in the Italian style

Carl Stamitz (1745-1801)
    symphonies, concertos, overtures,
    chamber music, string quartets,
    a few vocal works

Son of Johann; composer, violinist, and
violist; Mannheim composer

*William Billings (1746-1800)
    Psalms, hymns, writings

Most prominent composer in the New
America; also a singing teacher

Giuseppe Maria Cambini (1746-1825)
    10 operas, sacred and secular
    vocal works, 80 symphonies, 149
    string quartets, chamber music

Italian composer and violinist; very
popular and prolific in his day

*Domenico Cimarosa (1749-1801)
    65 operas, oratorios, masses,
    6 quartets, keyboard works

Italian composer; a central figure in opera
in the late 18th century; extraordinarily
successful in his day

*Lorenzo Da Ponte (1749-1838)

Italian librettist and poet; collaborated
with Mozart; moved to the US and was
professor at Columbia College in New
York; he was a controversial character

*Johann Wolfgang von Goethe
    (1749-1832)

German poet and writer; he was a literary
force behind Romanticism; composers
continue to set his works to music

*Antonio Salieri (1750-1825)
    46 operas, oratorios, masses,
    liturgical music, cantatas, 180
    canons, chamber music, arias,
    some orchestral music,
    pedagogical works

Italian composer and teacher; he
functioned in the transitional periods
between the galant and the classic and
then again between the classic and the
romantic; extremely successful

*Muzio Clementi (1752-1832)
    sonatas, chamber music,
    symphonies, pedagogical works

English composer of Italian birth;
keyboardist, teacher, music publisher,
and piano manufacturer

Johann Friedrich Reichardt (1752-1814)
    1500 songs, 32 operas, ballets,
    choral music, concertos, chamber
    music, keyboard works, writings

German composer and writer; prolific
and well-known

Niccolò Antonio Zingarelli (1752-1837)
    40 operas, sacred and secular
    vocal works, symphonies,
    chamber music, fugues

Italian composer and teacher;
conservative style

Franz Anton Hoffmeister (1754-1812)
    66 symphonies, stage works,
    chamber music, concertos

Austrian composer and music publisher

Vincente Martín y Soler (1754-1806)
    operas (serious and comic), vocal
    works, ballets

Spanish composer; important opera
composer in his day; collaborated with Da
Ponte

Giovanni Battista Viotti (1755-1824)
    29 violin concertos, string
    quartets, trios, duos, solos, a few
    keyboard and vocal works,
    writings

Italian composer and violinist; the most
important violinist after Tartini; he is
considered the founder of the 19th century
French school of violin technique

*Wolfgang Amadeus Mozart (1756-91)
    20 operas, piano concertos, other
    concertos, symphonies, sonatas
    choral music, chamber music
    songs, other vocal works

Exploited child prodigy; wrote in all
genres; best innovations were in opera;
he represents to many today the epitome
of the classic style

Ignaz Josef Pleyel (1757-1831)
    symphonies, concertos, sonatas,
    quartets, other chamber and
    orchestral music, a few stage
    and keyboard works, vocal works

Austrian composer, piano maker, and
publisher; he was most important for his
publishing house in Paris, publishing over
4000 works from 1795 to 1834

Carl Friedrich Zelter (1758-1832)
    cantatas, secular and sacred
    vocal works, songs, keyboard
    works, writings

German composer, teacher, and
conductor; most important for his vocal
works and his influence in Berlin

Maria Theresia von Paradis (1759-1824)
    2 piano concertos, piano works,
    2 operas, 3 cantatas,
    Singspiel, and songs

Pianist, organist, singer; blind from age 2;
knew Mozart; studied with Salieri; headed
a music school in Vienna for women

Jan Ladislav Dussek (1760-1812)
    vocal and stage works, concertos,
    sonatas, chamber music, writings

Czech composer and pianist; one of the
early touring concert pianists

Johann Rudolf Zumsteeg (1760-1802)
    13 stage works, ballads, songs,
    choral music, orchestral works

German composer and conductor;
admired for his text settings

Franz Xaver Süssmayr (1766-1803)
    30 stage works, masses, chamber
    music, 2 symphonies

Austrian composer; student of Mozart;
helped in the completion of Mozart's
Requiem

Nineteenth Century (Romantic): 1810s-1900

Romanticism was brewing in German Literature at the end of the 18th century. By the early 1810s, this new expressive art had made its way into music. Beethoven was the key figure who helped mold the older classical style

into the new romantic style. By the 1820s, this trend developed into new forms of dramaticism for music. Berlioz's *Symphonie Fantastique*, from 1830, changed musical style permanently and the rise of the conductor characterized this change.

Luigi Cherubini (1760-1842)
    38 dramatic works, masses,
    choral music, cantatas, sonatas,
    chamber music, pedagogical
    works

Italian composer, theorist, teacher, and
administrator working in Paris; he was a
dominant figure in French musical life,
especially in opera and education

Jean-François Le Sueur (1760-1837)
    stage works, writings

French composer and writer; important
to French music during and after the
Revolution

Johann Simon Mayr (1763-1845)
    68 dramatic works, oratorios,
    cantatas, masses, other vocal
    works, 2 symphonies, writings

Founder of Romantic Italian Opera;
German by birth; a central figure in
Italian opera before Rossini and after
Mozart

Etienne-Nicolas Méhul (1763-1817)
    31 operas, ballets, choral music,
    revolutionary songs, symphonies,
    a few chamber and keyboard
    works

French composer; contributed to the
genre of opéra comique; he was the most
important French composer of
symphonies in the early 19th century

*Prince Nikolaus Eszterházy (1765-1833)

Haydn's patron and employer after 1790

*Ludwig van Beethoven (1770-1827)
    9 symphonies, 32 piano sonatas,
    1 opera, string quartets, masses,
    concertos, arias, Lieder,
    overtures, other choral and
    chamber music

Instrumental in moving music towards Romanticism; he is an icon in our present culture; he established the heroic gesture in orchestral music

Antonie [Anton] Reicha (1770-1836)
    18 operas, choral music, vocal-
    orchestral works, symphonies,
    overtures, concertos, chamber
    music, piano works, writings

Czech composer; especially important as a theorist and teacher in Paris

Ferdinando Paer (1771-1839)
    55 operas, cantatas, oratorios,
    other vocal and chamber works

Italian composer and teacher; admired by Napoleon

Gaspare Spontini (1774-1851)
    24 operas, other dramatic works,
    songs, choral music, instrumental
    works, writings

Italian working in Paris; conductor; Empress Josephine's favorite musician; the central figure in French serious opera from 1800 to 1820

Adrien Boieldieu (1775-1834)
    at least 40 stage works, concertos,
    chamber music, choral music,
    piano works

French composer; he was the leading composer of opera in France during the early 19th century; a leader in opéra comique

*E. T. A. Hoffmann (1776-1822)
    writings, stage works, piano
    works, vocal works, some
    chamber and orchestral works

German writer and composer; writer of *The Nutcracker* fable; his writings epitomize Romanticism; also an artist

Johann Nepomuk Hummel (1778-1837)
    piano works, chamber music,
    orchestral works, operas, ballets,
    songs and other vocal works,
    pedagogical works

Austrian composer, pianist, teacher, and conductor; student of Mozart; very important during his day

Louise Reichardt (1779-1826)
    90 songs

Daughter of J. F. Reichardt; singing teacher; conducted women's chorus in Hamburg

John Field (1782-1837)
    7 piano concertos, chamber
    music, piano works

Irish composer and pianist; he originated the Romantic style of piano writing that is credited to Chopin; he invented the piano nocturne

Nicolò Paganini (1782-1840)
  violin-orchestral works, chamber music, violin solos, a few vocal works

Italian violinist and composer; he contributed significantly to the history of the violin and to the development of virtuosity

Georges Onslow (1784-1853)
  4 symphonies, 4 dramatic works, 35 string quartets, 34 string quintets, sonatas

French composer of English descent; Berlioz thought he would be Beethoven's successor—he was not

Ferdinand Ries (1784-1838)
  piano works, chamber music, 8 symphonies, overtures, concertos, 54 songs

German composer, pianist, and copyist; student of Beethoven

Louis Spohr (1784-1859)
  13 stage works, 10 symphonies, many concertos, solo violin works, string quartets, chamber music, choral music, songs, writings

German composer, conductor, and violinist; he used Leitmotifs in his operas before Wagner did; prolific

Frédéric Kalkbrenner (1785-1849)
  concertos, chamber music, piano works

French composer, pianist, and teacher of German birth; recognized throughout Europe for his performances

*Carl Maria von Weber (1786-1826)
  German opera, other dramatic works, cantatas, concertos, piano works, songs, 2 symphonies, writings

Founder of German Romantic Opera; studied with Michael Haydn

Giacomo Meyerbeer (1791-1864)
  17 operas, other dramatic works, choral music, songs, a few instrumental works

The leading composer of French Grand Opera; Jewish, and the object of Wagner's anti-Semitic writings in 1850

*Gioachino Rossini (1792-1868)
  39 operas, choral music, vocal works, 2 sinfonia

The most famous composer in the early 19th century in Vienna; composed mostly choral music and operas

Ignaz Moscheles (1794-1870)
  piano works, 1 symphony, piano concertos, chamber music, songs

German composer, pianist, teacher, and conductor of Czech birth; important as pianist during the time of Schumann and Mendelssohn

Saverio Mercadante (1795-1870)
    59 operas, ballets, choral music,
    cantatas, hymns, concertos,
    orchestral and chamber works

Italian composer and teacher; during his day he was as important as Donizetti, Bellini, and Verdi; prolific in most genres

*Gaetano Donizetti (1797-1848)
    70 operas, symphonies,
    chamber music, 100 songs,
    choral music

Student of Mayr; Verdi's immediate forerunner in serious Italian opera; prolific composer of all genres

*Franz Schubert (1797-1828)
    over 600 Lieder, 9 symphonies,
    chamber music, piano works,
    13 operas, choral music

Created a genre of artistic and dramatic Lieder; expansive melodies; frequent modulations; many unfinished works

*Vincenzo Bellini (1801-35)
    10 serious operas

Italian opera composer; created dramas with extreme passion, action, and emotion

*Hector Berlioz (1803-69)
    operas, choral music, chamber
    music, tone poems, symphonies,
    works of untraditional genres,
    vocal works, writings

French composer, conductor, writer, and innovator; he was the leading French musician in his day; his works embody the notions of Romanticism

Louise Farrenc (1804-75)
    many piano works,
    2 overtures, 3 symphonies,
    chamber music

French composer, pianist, teacher, and scholar; the most esteemed French female professor in the 19th century

*Mikhail Glinka (1804-57)
    9 operas, chamber music,
    orchestral works, piano works,
    vocal works

The father of Russian music; European trained

*Fanny Mendelssohn Hensel (1805-47)
    an overture, 250 Lieder
    28 choral works, chamber music

Had the same training as Felix; she was discouraged from composing; married, then published more; her house was a center for intellectuals and culture

*Felix Mendelssohn (1809-47)
    symphonies, concertos,
    chamber music, Lieder.
    piano and organ works

Early romantic; conservative style; important as a conductor; revived Bach's music

Félicien David (1810-76)
7 stage works, symphonies, tone poems, choral music, oratorios, other chamber, piano, and vocal works

French composer; after Berlioz, the only other composer to do something highly original in the symphonic genre; he favored oriental topics

*Robert Schumann (1810-56)
4 symphonies, Lieder, chamber music, piano works, concertos, 1 not-so-great opera

Important as critic, editor, and composer; center of musical life; lost his sanity at a young age

*Frédéric François Chopin (1810-49)
piano concertos, chamber music that involved a piano, sonatas,

Polish/French composer and pianist; he innovated new piano techniques; he is more famous today than during his lifetime; known for his character pieces

*Franz Liszt (1811-86)
tone poems, dramatic works, Lieder, concertos, piano works, vocal works, writings

Virtuoso pianist; conductor; author; supporter of Wagner; innovator in musical form, aesthetics, and harmonies; inventor of the orchestral tone poem

Ambroise Thomas (1811-96)
20 operas, ballets, songs, vocal works, chamber music, orchestral and pedagogical works

French composer; important to French opera

*Giuseppe Verdi (1813-1901)
the
26 operas, choral music

The leading Italian opera composer of

19th century; became a national hero of Italy

*Richard Wagner (1813-83)
operas, music dramas, 1 poor symphony, writings

Creator of German Music Drama; conductor, writer, musical innovator; desired music of the future; Anti-Semite; profoundly influenced Western harmony; strove for an endless melody

Josephine Lang (1815-80)
150 songs, piano works

German composer and singer; one of the most published women composers in the 19th century

Niels Gade (1817-90)
stage works, choral music, symphonies, chamber music, piano works, songs

Danish composer, conductor, violinist, and teacher; he was ranked with Brahms by his contemporary public

*Charles Gounod (1818-93)
    12 operas, oratorios
    masses, much choral music,
    piano works

French prolific composer

Jacques Offenbach (1819-80)
    97 dramatic works, vocal works,
    ballets, dance music, works for
    cello

The founder of Opéra bouffe; introduced the *can-can*

*Clara Wieck Schumann (1819-96)
    Lieder, piano concerto

Virtuoso pianist; wife of Robert Schumann; close friend of Brahms

Pauline Viardot-Garcia (1821-1910)
    5 stage works, choral music,
    vocal, instrumental and piano
    works

French composer, teacher, singer, and pianist; student of Liszt

*César Franck (1822-90)
    4 stage works, choral music,
    orchestral works, songs, chamber
    music, piano and organ works

French nationalist composer, teacher, and organist

Joachim Raff (1822-82)
    stage works, choral-orchestral
    works, 11 symphonies, chamber
    music, other vocal and piano
    works, writings

German composer, teacher, and writer; ranked with Brahms during his day; associated with Liszt

*Anton Bruckner (1824-96)
    symphonies, organ works,
    choral music

German, composer and organist; follower of Wagner; known for his large orchestrations

Carl Reinecke (1824-1910)
    piano works, stage and vocal
    works, chamber music,
    symphonies, overtures, writings,
    concertos

German composer, teacher, pianist, writer, and conductor

*Bedrich Smetana (1824-84)
    tone poems, operas

Czech composer; established Czech opera in the 19th c.; nationalist

Eduard Hanslick (1825-1904)
    writings

German music critic and writer; he is considered the first professional music critic; we learn a great deal about 19th-century aesthetics from his writings

*Johann Strauss (1825-99)
    Viennese operettas

Called the "Waltz-King"

*Stephen Foster (1826-64)
    songs

American songwriter

Louis Moreau Gottschalk (1829-69)
    symphonies, concertos, piano
    works, a few operas and vocal
    works

American composer and virtuoso pianist; one of the most significant American 19th-century musicians; well-known in Europe

Anton Rubinstein (1829-94)
    20 stage works, concertos,
    piano and choral works, chamber
    music, songs, writings

Russian composer and virtuoso pianist; Founder of the St. Petersburg Conservatory in 1862

Joseph Joachim (1831-1907)
    overtures, concertos, chamber
    music, pedagogical works

Hungarian violinist, composer, conductor, and teacher; toured with Clara Schumann; friends with Brahms

Aleksandr Borodin (1833-87)
    symphonies, string quartets,
    operas, vocal and piano works

One of the Russian Mighty Five; a chemist by profession

*Johannes Brahms (1833-97)
    4 symphonies, concertos,
    choral music, chamber music,
    Lieder, German Requiem,
    piano works other orchestral
    works

Known as the classic-romantic; never wrote an opera; strong knowledge of the musical past; one of the first editors of Bach's music; conductor, pianist; friends with the Schumanns

Nikolay Rubinstein (1835-81)

Russian composer, pianist, conductor, and teacher; brother of Anton; he founded the Moscow Conservatory

*Camille Saint-Saëns (1835-1921)
    21 stage works, choral music,
    songs, orchestral works,
    chamber music, piano works,
    writings

French composer, pianist, organist, and writer

César Cui (1835-1918)
    15 stage works, choral music,
    orchestral and piano works,
    chamber music, songs, writings

One of the Russian Mighty Five; of French descent

Mily Balakirev (1837-1910)
    2 stage works, choral music, orchestral and piano works, songs

One of the Russian Mighty Five; one of the more professionally trained musicians of the five

*Georges Bizet (1838-75)
    28 dramatic works, piano works, songs

French composer who created a new type of serious French opera

*Modest Musorgsky (1839-81)
    9 operas, orchestral works, piano works, Russian songs and cycles

One of the Russian Mighty Five; most famous of the 5 today; his music is rooted in Russian folksong and lore

*John Knowles Paine (1839-1906)
    4 stage works, choral music, songs, orchestral works, piano and chamber works, writings

American; organist, composer; teacher of the new generation of American composers; Harvard's first professor of music

*Piotr Il'yich Tchaikovsky (1840-93)
    26 stage works, 6 symphonies, symphonic poems, concertos, choral and chamber music, songs, writings

Not a proclaimed nationalist; Western trained; emotional; conductor; conservative harmonic language; popular today with our public

Emmanuel Chabrier (1841-94)
    10 operas, songs, vocal and orchestral works, piano works

French composer and pianist; Ravel's main influence; important for his piano works and imaginative stage works

*Antonín Dvorák (1841-1904)
    9 symphonies, choral music, chamber music, piano works concertos, orchestral works, songs

The most famous of the Czech composers; lived in USA; influenced by African-American music and culture

Jules Massenet (1842-1912)
    25 operas, 280 songs, orchestral works, piano works, symphonic poems

French composer; prolific and versatile

Arthur Sullivan (1842-1900)
    stage works, choral-orchestral works, other orchestral works, hymns, chamber music, songs

English composer and conductor; his comic operas are still popular today (Gilbert and Sullivan operas)

Edvard Grieg (1843-1907)
  concertos, orchestral works,
  stage works, songs, choral music,
  chamber music, piano works

The most important Norwegian composer during his day

*Nikolay Rimsky-Korsakov (1844-1908)
  symphonies, 20 stage works,
  chamber music, choral music,
  symphonic poems, piano works,
  songs, writings

One of the Russian Mighty Five; important as a teacher; conductor; wrote an orchestration treatise

*Gabriel Fauré (1845-1924)
  stage works, songs, choral music,
  vocal and orchestral works,
  chamber music, piano works,
  writings

French composer, teacher, and keyboardist; he foreshadowed modern tonality and style; extremely important as a teacher

Vincent d'Indy (1851-1931)
  tone poems, symphonies, operas,
  songs, keyboard works, writings

French composer, theorist and writer; Franck's leading pupil; used folksong

Charles Villiers Stanford (1852-1924)
  oratorios, cantatas, choral and
  vocal music, symphonies,
  concertos, songs, keyboard works,
  chamber music, stage works,
  writings

British composer, conductor, writer, and teacher; he made important contributions to English church music

*Leos Janácek (1854-1928)
  12 stage works, orchestral works,
  chamber music, choral music,
  keyboard works, folksong
  arrangements and editions

Czech composer; ethnomusicologist; influenced by folk music

Engelbert Humperdinck (1854-1921)
  stage music, choral music, songs,
  a few instrumental works, writings

German composer, critic, and teacher; close to Wagner

*John Philip Sousa (1854-1932)
  over 100 marches, vocal works

American; leader of the U.S. Marine Band in 1880

Ernest Chausson (1855-99)
  tone poems, 6 stage works,
  chamber and vocal works

French composer; admirer of Franck and Wagner

Cécile Chaminade (1857-1944)
   200 piano works, chamber music,
   opera comique, 2 concertos
   songs

French composer and pianist; most of her works were published

* Edward Elgar (1857-1934)
   symphonies, overtures, 9 stage
   works, choral music chamber
   music, piano works, writings

English composer; received international acclaim; not folksong oriented

Ruggiero Leoncavallo (1857-1919)
   12 operas, 10 operettas, songs,
   2 libretti, a few keyboard works

Italian composer and librettist; strove for realism in his dramatic works

*Giacomo Puccini (1858-1924)
   10 operas, vocal works, a few
   instrumental and chamber works

Italian opera composer; gift for delicate melodies; strove for realism; the most successful Italian opera composer after Verdi

Cecil Sharp (1859-1924)
   folksong editions, writings

English composer; collector and editor of folksongs

*Hugo Wolf (1860-1903)
   250 Lieder, 1 opera

Wrote mostly Lieder; influenced by Wagner

*Gustav Mahler (1860-1911)
   5 orchestral song cycles. Lieder,
   10 symphonies, chamber music

The epitome of Romanticism; large programmatic symphonies, orchestral Lieder; conductor in Europe and the USA

Twentieth Century: 1900-2000

The twentieth century was diverse in musical styles, trends, and forms. There is no one stylistic trait that unifies the century. The two primary trends in the early century, Impressionism and Expressionism, are listed separately below. Most composers wrote in a variety of styles, experimenting with many techniques. Therefore, the majority of composers belong in the general list.

Impressionism: The First Modern Style, 1890s+

Isaac Albeniz (1860-1909)
   piano and dramatic works,
   orchestral works, songs

Spanish composer and pianist; very important to Spain

*Claude Debussy (1862-1918)
    piano works, chamber music,
    tone poems, 5 operas, songs

French composer and pianist; inventor of musical impressionism; influential modern composers

Frederick Delius (1862-1934)
    9 stage works, orchestral, choral
    and chamber music, songs

English composer of German descent; used impressionism

Pietro Mascagni (1863-1945)
    operas, songs, other vocal and
    instrumental works

Italian composer and conductor; he became the official composer of the Fascist regime in the 1930s

Erik Satie (1866-1925)
    15 dramatic works, songs, piano
    works, writings

Not an impressionist, but a leader in new French aesthetics on which impressionism was built; innovator

*Maurice Ravel (1875-1937)
    2 operas, ballets, orchestral,
    vocal and piano works

French composer; extremely versatile; innovator in pianistic style; expert orchestrator

Ottorino Respighi (1879-1936)
    11 stage works, concertos, tone
    poems, some vocal and piano
    works

Italian composer; used impressionism

*Nadia Boulanger (1887-1979)

Important teacher of composers in the 20th c.; most American composers studied with her; also a conductor and composer

Lili Boulanger (1893-1918)
    opera, choral music,
    cantatas, orchestral works_

French composer; first woman to win the Prix de Rome, 1913; sister of Nadia

Les Six (The famous group of six French composers):

Louis Durey (1888-1979)
    5 stage works, orchestral works,
    chamber music, piano works,
    film scores

Turned communist in 1936; not talked about much in music history; anti-USA

Arthur Honegger (1892-1955)
    choral music, chamber music,
    5 symphonies

From Switzerland; admired Bach

Darius Milhaud (1892-1974)   Friends with Satie; used polytonality
    operas, films, children's music,
    choral music, organ works

Germaine Tailleferre (1892-1983)   French composer; too modest; beautiful
    12 operas, 4 ballets, film and   music
    television scores, orchestral
    works, choral music, songs,
    chamber music, piano works,
    writings

Georges Auric (1899-1983)   French composer; by age 15 he had
    songs, piano works, 1 opera,   written over 200 works; wrote for French
    ballets, chamber music   film

*Francis Poulenc (1899-1963)   French composer; delicate and sometimes
    piano works, choral music,   irreverent style; harmonically charming
    concertos, chamber music

Composers Who Innovated Atonality

*Charles Ives (1874-1954)   American; probably
    songs, piano works, orchestral   the most innovative,
    sets and other works, symphonies,   original, and creative
    choral music, band music,   of all 20th c. composers; worked virtually
    chamber music, writings   in isolation; made a living in insurance

*Arnold Schoenberg (1874-1951)   The father of 12-tone music; important as
    4 operas, symphonies, choral   an innovator; teacher of Webern and
    and chamber music, songs,   Berg
    canons, piano works, writings

*Anton von Webern (1883-1945)   Student of Schoenberg; known for his
    symphonies, other orchestral   musical brevity and clarity of texture;
    works, chamber and choral   pointillism; wrote no operas
    music, songs, writings

*Alban Berg (1885-1935)   Student of Schoenberg; expressive
    opera, orchestral works, songs,   language; often atonal
    concertos, chamber music
    writings

General List of Twentieth-Century Composers

One cannot fathom how many accomplished composers are living today. I suggest you visit the website entitled, the "Living Composers Project" at **http://www.composers21.com/?** The website allows you to search by country or name.

*Richard Strauss (1864-1949)
    Symphonic Poems, 15 operas,
    150 Lieder, other stage works,
    orchestral works, chamber music,
    piano works, writings

Composer of tone poems and some of the first modern operas; accomplished conductor

Aleksandr Glazunov (1865-1936)
    symphonies, concertos,
    stage works, chamber music
    choral music, writings

Pupil of Rimsky-Korsakov; the last of the Russian nationalists

Paul Dukas (1865-1935)
    surviving works include a few
    orchestral, choral, piano, and
    vocal works

French composer, teacher, and critic; only allowed a few of his works to be published

Carl Nielsen (1865-1931)
    symphonies, operas, piano
    works, concertos, chamber
    music, songs

Danish; prolific and important to the history of Scandinavian music

*Jean Sibelius (1865-1957)
    tone poems, 7 symphonies,
    concertos, chamber music

Finnish; his later music is more modern

Ferruccio Busoni (1866-1924)
    6 stage works, orchestral works,
    vocal-orchestral works, piano
    works, songs, chamber music,
    writings

Important Italian composer; advocated moving away from "the tyranny of major and minor keys"; yet, his music sounds more conservative than his talk

*Amy Marcy Cheney Beach (1867-1944)
    1 opera, vocal-orchestral works,
    chamber music, keyboard works,
    choral works, 130 songs

American composer and pianist; very successful in Europe; conservative style; wrote scholarly articles

Enrique Granados (1867-1916)
    piano music, stage works

Catalan composer, teacher and pianist He is a representative composer of 19th-century Spain

*Scott Joplin (1867/68-1917)
    ragtime, 1 opera, marches,
    waltzes

American; popularized ragtime

Hans Pfitzner (1869-1949)
    8 stage works, chamber music,
    orchestral works, writings

The leading conservative German composer; also a conductor

*Ralph Vaughan Williams (1872-1958)
    symphonies, choral music,
    chamber music, 10 stage works,
    orchestral and band music,
    songs, carols, hymns, writings

Became the leader in English music; collector and editor of folksongs and hymns, musical editor of the English Hymnal; teacher and conductor

* Aleksandr Skryabin (1872-1915)
    tone poems, piano works,
    3 symphonies, writings

Influenced by chromaticism and impressionism; complex original harmonic language; virtuoso pianist

Max Reger (1873-1916)
    choral music, chamber music,
    symphonic poems, piano works,
    editions, writings

German composer; Post-Wagnerian harmony; extreme chromaticism; master of counterpoint

*Sergei Rachmaniov (1873-1943)
    symphonies, piano concertos,
    symphonic poems, 6 operas,
    choral music, piano works, songs

Not interested in nationalism; master of melody; virtuoso pianist; toured the USA

*Gustav Holst (1874-1934)
    orchestral works, 15 stage works,
    choral, chamber works, songs

English; influenced by folksong and Hindu mysticism; original composer and important teacher

*Manuel de Falla (1876-1946)
    orchestral works, 19 stage works,
    vocal works, chamber music,
    writings

The principal Spanish composer of the 20th c.; used Spanish popular and folk music; earned international fame

*Béla Bartok (1881-1945)
    concertos, piano works,
    chamber music, 3 stage works,
    orchestral works, choral works,
    songs, many editions and writings

Hungarian composer and pianist; important ethnomusicologist; known for his rhythmic music; he incorporated his own native folk music into his compositions

Karol Szymanowski (1882-1937)
    6 stage works, orchestral and
    vocal-orchestral works, songs,
    piano works, chamber music,
    writings

Polish composer; the central figure in
Polish music in the early 20th century

*Igor Stravinsky (1882-1971)
    symphonies, ballets,
    operas, chamber music,
    choral music, piano works

One of the most versatile and interesting
composers of the 20th c.; rhythmic style;
harmonically interesting

*Zoltán Kodály (1882-1967)
    7 stage works, choral music,
    orchestral suites, songs, chamber
    music, pedagogical works, writings

Hungarian; ethnomusicologist, music
educator; created movable 'do' solfege
system

Gian Francesco Malipiero (1882-1973)
    35 operas, 6 ballets, vocal and
    orchestral works, piano works,
    chamber music, editions, writings

Italian composer and musicologist;
original and inventive

*Edgard Varèse (1883-1965)
    orchestral works, non-traditional
    genres, stages works, choral
    music, writings

French-American; wrote non-tonal music,
focusing on elements other than pitch;
innovative; took interest in electronic
music and the idea of organized sound as
music

Charles T. Griffes (1884-1920)
    6 stage works, chamber music,
    songs, piano works, a few
    orchestral works

American composer and pianist;
interested in ethnic music

Luigi Russolo (1885-1947)
    works for his instruments are
    mostly lost; his published writings
    survive

Italian inventor, painter, and composer;
he created a riot in Milan in 1913 when
he demonstrated his new instruments that
were to produce machine noises of daily
experiences

*Heitor Villa-Lobos (1887-1959)
    12 dramatic works, choral music,
    orchestral and vocal works,
    chamber music, piano works,
    writings

Brazilian composer and cellist

Florence Price (1887-1953)
symphonies, concertos, choral
music, vocal and piano works,
songs

American composer; adapted Juba
folk dance and idioms of black spirituals;
the first African-American woman to win
widespread fame as a symphonic
composer; even so, she was omitted from
the *New Grove Dictionary* in 1980.

Frank Martin (1890-1974)
stage works, choral music, vocal
works, symphonies, orchestral
works, chamber music, writings

Swiss composer of French descent

Cole Porter (1891-1964)
musicals, songs

American songwriter and composer

*Sergei Prokofiev (1891-1953)
symphonies, concertos, songs,
operas, film scores, chamber
music, dramatic music, ballets,
choral music, piano works

Russian composer and pianist; important
as a Russian voice in Western culture

Alois Hába (1893-1973)
1 opera, orchestral and vocal
works, string quartets, piano
works, chamber music, writings

Czech composer, theorist and teacher

Walter Piston (1894-1976)
chamber music, symphonies,
other orchestral music, writings

American composer and teacher; neo-
classic and craft-oriented

*Paul Hindemith (1895-1963)
19 dramatic works, orchestral,
chamber music, choral works
songs, chamber music, writings

German conductor, teacher, author
and composer; wrote music for the
practicing musician; *Gebrauchsmusik*

Carl Orff (1895-1982)
19 stage works, a few other
choral works, writings

German composer and educationist;
indebted to folksong (Bavarian); wrote a
collection of graded material for children
for use in schools

*William Grant Still (1895-1978)
5 symphonies, 9 operas, ballets,
vocal and instrumental works,
songs

American composer; the first African-
American composer to have his symphony
performed by a leading orchestra; the
first black American to conduct a major
orchestra; the first black American
to write for radio, TV, and films; he
incorporated folk idioms, jazz, and
spirituals

Roger Sessions (1896-1985)
    8 symphonies (rarely performed)
    3 stage works, concertos, a few
    chamber and choral works,
    writings

American composer, theorist, and teacher; atonal mostly; intense and dissonant

Howard Hanson (1896-1981)
    6 symphonies, 2 ballets,
    opera, chamber music

American composer, teacher, and conductor of Swedish ancestry; neo-romantic style

Virgil Thomson (1896-1989)
    3 operas, orchestral works,
    2 ballets, orchestral and band
    works, choral music, vocal works,
    chamber music, film scores,
    writings

American composer and critic; influenced by hymnody; his style foreshadowed minimalism

Ira Gershwin (1896-1983)
    lyrics for songs and musicals

Brother of George; used the pen name Arthur Francis early in his career (Arthur was their brother and Francis was their sister)

Henry Cowell (1897-1965)
    21 symphonies, other orchestral
    works, choral music, chamber
    music, piano works, stage works,
    writings

American composer, teacher, and writer; innovator of indeterminacy (chance music); his experimental enthusiasm helped to create modern music

*George Gershwin (1898-1937)
    30 stage works, film scores,
    songs, instrumental and piano
    works

Influential American composer, pianist, and conductor who worked in Hollywood; he successfully fused jazz and pop music into the classical style and concert hall

Hanns Eisler (1898-1962)
    choral-orchestral works, vocal
    works, orchestral works, 38 stage
    works, film scores, writings

German composer; pupil of Schoenberg; politically committed composer in East Germany Post WWII; fought against capitalism and fascism

Roy Harris (1898-1979)
    14 symphonies, other orchestral
    and band works, chamber and
    choral music, dramatic works,
    songs, writings

American composer; influenced by folk music

*Duke Ellington (1899-1974)

American jazz composer, band-leader and pianist; Created a unique style of big-band jazz; one of the first African-American composers to cross races with his music

*Carlos Chávez (1899-1978)
    7 stage works, symphonies,
    choral and vocal music, songs,
    instrumental works, writings

Mexican composer, conductor, teacher, writer, and government official; extremely important to Mexican culture

Randall Thompson (1899-1984)
    choral and vocal works,
    2 operas, orchestral and
    chamber works

American composer and teacher

Silvestre Revueltas (1899-1940)
    ballets, orchestral music, string
    quartets, chamber music, songs,
    film scores

Mexican composer and violinist of international acclaim; he is representative of the "mestizo realism" movement that drew upon the popular culture of Mexico

*Aaron Copland (1900-90)
    2 operas, 3 symphonies, 6 ballets,
    8 film scores, choral music,
    piano and chamber music,
    concertos, writings

Most popular American composer of the 20th c.; teacher, conductor, author; his music still has a special appeal to the American public

Ernst Krenek (1900-91)
    20 operas, other stage works,
    choral music, orchestral works,
    symphonies, vocal works, piano
    and chamber works, writings

American composer of Austrian birth; trained in Vienna

Kurt Weill (1900-50)
    30 stage works, film and radio
    scores, orchestral works, songs,
    chamber music

German opera composer in Berlin; moved to the USA, composed on Broadway in New York City

*Louis Armstrong (1900/01-71)
    publications for trumpet

African-American jazz musician who revolutionized jazz; singer, band-leader, and trumpeter

Harry Partch (1901-74)
    works for his instruments,
    various non-traditional genres,
    writings

American innovator; inventor of new instruments; developed a 43-note scale

Ruth Crawford Seeger (1901-53)
　　chamber music, vocal and
　　orchestral works, a few piano
　　works, folksong transcriptions

American composer and folk-music
specialist; married to musicologist Charles
Seeger; most popular among modernists
in the 1920s and 30s

Maurice Duruflé (1902-1986)

French composer and organist; not very
prolific; influenced by chant

William Walton (1902-83)
　　symphonies, choral music,
　　chamber music

English composer; a central figure for
England

Aram Khachaturian (1903-78)
　　dramatic works, a few vocal,
　　chamber and orchestral works

Armenian composer; one of the pillars of
the Russian school of composers

Goffredo Petrassi (1904-2003)
　　5 dramatic works, orchestral
　　works, choral and chamber
　　music, writings

Italian composer and teacher; after
Dallapiccola, he is the most important
composer in Italy during his day

Luigi Dallapiccola (1904-1975)
　　5 dramatic works, film scores,
　　choral music, vocal works,
　　chamber music, writings

Italian composer, pianist, and writer; the
principal innovator in Italy in the
20th century

Michael Tippet (1905-98)
　　10 stage works, choral music,
　　orchestral works, chamber
　　music, piano works, writings

One of England's most important and
original composers; favored neo-
classicism

Louise Talma (1906-1996)
　　1 opera, choral music, vocal

　　works, orchestral and piano
　　works

American composer; exponent of
serialism

*Dimitri Shostakovich (1906-1975)
　　15 symphonies, operas, ballets,
　　orchestral works, chamber music,
　　songs, piano works, writings

Versatile; the most important Russian
composer working in Russia in his day

*Elliott Carter (b. 1908)
　　chamber music, string quartets,
　　orchestral and stage works,
　　writings

American composer, teacher; innovative
treatment of rhythm and form;
continuous mutation

*Olivier Messiaen (1908-92)
    orchestral and vocal works,
    piano and organ works, writings,
    instrumental and tape works

French composer, author, and organist;
incorporated sounds of nature; innovator
in rhythm; the first to advocate total
serialism

*Samuel Barber (1910-81)
    operas, ballets, orchestral works,
    choral music, vocal works,
    chamber music, songs

American composer and accomplished
singer; child prodigy and gifted melodist;
continued with a successful conservative
tonality in the midst of 20th c. musical
experimentations

William Schuman (1910-92)
    ballets, operas, orchestral works,
    symphonies, concertos, band
    works, chamber music, vocal
    works, writings

American composer and teacher;
used borrowed subjects

Pierre Schaeffer (1910-95)
    works for tape alone, writings

French composer, theorist, writer, and
teacher; the innovator of musique
concrete

Gian Carlo Menotti (b. 1911)
    operas, ballets, concertos,
    orchestral and vocal works,
    writings

American composer of Italian birth;
important as a modern opera composer

Alan Hovhaness (1911-2000)
    operas, ballets, symphonies,
    orchestral works, chamber music,
    choral music, piano works

American composer of Armenian and
Scottish descent; Armenian influence in
his music

*John Cage (1912-92)
    many works of non-traditional
    genre, piano works, vocal works,
    chamber music, tape music,
    writings

American composer and philosopher;
most innovative composer of the 20th
century; changed the definition of music;
used indeterminacy; he was the center of
avant-garde music in the mid-20th century

Conlon Nancarrow (1912-97)
    piano works, player-piano
    works, chamber music, a few
    orchestral works

Mexican composer of American birth;
interested in jazz, African music, and
music of India; used piano player rolls to
play his rhythmically complex pieces

Norman Dello Joio (b. 1913)
    stage and choral works, chamber
    and orchestral music

American composer, organist, teacher;
studied with Hindemith; considers himself
an arch conservative

Henry Brant (b. 1913)
    works with spatial separation,
    concertos, chamber music, vocal
    works, film scores

American composer of Canadian birth; a leader in spatial music

Witold Lutoslawski (1913-94)
    symphonies, concertos, vocal
    works, chamber music

Polish composer and a leader in aleatoric (chance) music

*Benjamin Britten (1913-76)
    17 operas, choral music, chamber
    music, orchestral works, vocal
    music, incidental music, writings

Most prolific and best-known English composer of the 20th c.; kept opera alive in English speaking countries

George Perle (b. 1915)
    orchestral works, chamber music,
    vocal works, writings

American composer and theorist; retained tonal centers in his 12-tone music

Vincent Persichetti (1915-87)
    orchestral works, choral and
    chamber music, band music,
    piano works, songs

American composer, pianist, and conductor

*Milton Babbitt (b. 1916)
    orchestral and chamber works,
    vocal works, works with tape,
    writings

American composer, teacher, writer; used serialism; he denied the importance of his audience

Alberto Ginastera (1916-1983)
    ballets, operas, chamber music,
    choral, orchestral and vocal
    works

Argentine composer and pianist

Ulysses Kay (1917-95)
    orchestral and vocal works,
    choral music, dramatic works,
    chamber music

African-American composer; not folk-oriented; favored neo-classicism

Lou Harrison (1917-2003)
    stage works, orchestral and vocal
    works, chamber music, writings

American composer and teacher; favored the gamelan

George Rochberg (b. 1918)
    orchestral works, symphonies,
    vocal works, chamber music,

American composer and teacher who helped revive tonality in the 1970s

*Leonard Bernstein (1918-90)
    dramatic works, film scores,
    chamber and choral music, songs,
    filmed lectures and documentaries

American conductor, composer, teacher, author, pianist; most influential American musician of the 20th c.; brought classical music to the public via various media

Louis Barron (1920-89)
    film scores, electronic works

Composer of the first commercially released film to feature an entirely electronic soundtrack; a pioneer in electo-acoustic music; John Cage used the Barron studio for his first tape work in 1953; husband of Bebe Barron until the 1970s

Ralph Shapey (1921-2002)
    symphonies, vocal and orchestral
    works, chamber music, piano
    works

American composer, conductor, and teacher; used syllables in organized sound structures; united avant-garde and romantic aesthetics

Lukas Foss (b. 1922)
    dramatic and vocal works,
    orchestral works, chamber music,
    writings

American composer, conductor, and pianist of German birth; recognized for his experiments with improvisation and aleatoric (chance) music.

*Iannis Xenakis (b. 1922)
    orchestral works, choral music,
    chamber music, music with tape,
    writings

French composer of Greek parentage and Romanian birth; advocated Stochastic music (music based on mathematical calculations)

Ned Rorem (b. 1923)
    songs, operas, choral music,
    chamber and instrumental works,
    writings

American composer, poet, and author

*György Ligeti (b. 1923)
    electronic works, choral music,
    chamber music, orchestral works,
    writings

Austrian composer of Hungarian birth; wrote textural music with sound blocks

Luigi Nono (1924-1991)
    stage works, electronic music,
    orchestral and chamber music,
    vocal works, writings

Italian composer, conductor, and teacher; innovative and modern

Luciano Berio (1925-2003)
    dramatic works, orchestral works,
    vocal and chamber music, tape
    music, writings

Important Italian composer, conductor,
and teacher; advocated new tonalities and
techniques; his recent death leaves Italy
lacking internationally famous composers

*Pierre Boulez (b. 1925)
    orchestral, piano and vocal
    works, chamber music, writings

French composer, author, and conductor;
advocated total serialism; he said, "all art
of the past must be destroyed"; post-
modern

Bebe Barron (b. 1926)
    film scores, electronic works

Composer of the first commercially
released film to feature an entirely
electronic soundtrack; a pioneer in electo-
acoustic music; John Cage used the
Barron studio for his first tape work in
1953; she was married to Louis Barron
until the 1970s

Hans Werner Henze (b. 1926)
    operas, ballets, incidental music,
    symphonies, orchestral and vocal
    works, concertos, choral music,
    chamber music, string quartets,
    writings

German composer who created a fusion
of past musical traditions and new trends;
uses traditional genres

Ben Johnston (b. 1926)
    stage works, vocal and orchestral
    works, piano works, writings

American, microtonal composer;
studied with Partch and Cage

Earle Brown (b. 1926)
    piano works, tape music,
    chamber music, writings

American composer; first to use open
form; a leading representative of the Cage
school in the 1950s

Morton Feldman (1926-87)
    piano works, chamber music,
    orchestral and vocal works

American composer; also a representative
of the Cage school in the 1950s

Betsy Jolas (b. 1926)
    stage works, vocal and choral
    works, orchestral and chamber
    music, piano works

French composer

Carlisle Floyd (b. 1926)
    operas, chamber music, piano
    works, educational music

American composer; one of the foremost
composers of opera in the USA today

Thea Musgrave (b. 1928)
    stage works, orchestral and
    choral music, chamber and
    vocal works, sonatas, concertos,
    madrigals

Scottish composer; uses traditional genres
in a modern context

T. J. [Thomas Jefferson] Anderson
    (b. 1928); orchestral works,
    band and chamber music,
    vocal and piano works

African-American composer; uses Jazz
and post-Webern styles

*Karlheinz Stockhausen (b. 1928)
    works for tape, choral music,
    piano works, songs, electronic
    music, writings

German composer, teacher, conductor,
and theorist; he helped to pioneer
electronic music and new forms of
modern notation; he has been one of the
most important musical innovators in the
20th century, post WWII

*George Crumb (b. 1929)
    vocal works, chamber music,
    string quartets, sonatas, madrigals

American composer; most popular for
expressing despair during the Vietnam
War (1962-73)

Jerry Goldsmith (1929-2004)
    Film and TV scores

American composer

Stephen Sondheim (b. 1930)
    musicals

American composer

Mauricio Kagel (b. 1931)
    film and radio scores, choral
    music, multi-media works, vocal
    works, stage works, chamber
    music, writings

Argentine composer, filmmaker,
dramatist and performer; self taught as a
composer

Sofia Gubaidulina (b. 1931)
    orchestral works, choral and
    chamber music, concertos

Allowed to travel to the West in 1986;
works have spiritual connotations;
believes music has mystical properties

Isao Tomita (b. 1932)
    film and TV scores, stage works,
    electronic works

Japanese; composer of electronic music

*John Williams (b. 1932)
    80 film scores, orchestral works

American composer and conductor

Pauline Oliveros (b. 1932)
    dramatic works, multi-media
    works, instrumental and vocal
    works, electronic and tape music

American composer; accomplished tape-music composer

Morton Subotnick (b. 1933)
    orchestral and vocal works, tape
    music, writings

American composer and teacher; accomplished tape-music composer; his 1966 composition, *Silver Apples of the Moon* was the first electronic piece to be commissioned by a recording company

*Krzysztof Penderecki (b. 1933)
    dramatic works, vocal and
    orchestral works, tape music,
    chamber music

Polish composer; wrote textural music using sound blocks; his atonal music has public appeal

Henryk Gorecki (b. 1933)
    symphonies, vocal and orchestral
    works, chamber and choral
    music, piano works

Polish composer; neo-tonal; his recent works focus on tonal consonance

Fisher Tull (1934-94)
    orchestral, chamber, and vocal
    works

American composer, teacher, and conductor

Mario Davidovsky (b. 1934)
    orchestral works, electronic
    and tape works, chamber music,
    string quartets, vocal works

American composer of Argentine origin; known for his works that combine live performance with recorded electronic sounds

Peter Maxwell Davies (b. 1934)
    dramatic works, choral music,
    vocal and orchestral works,
    piano works, chamber music,
    writings

British composer; known for his avant-garde music in England

Alfred Schnittke (1934-98)
    8 symphonies, concertos,
    chamber music

Known for his Russian film music; moved to Germany; called his style polystylistic, incorporating styles from the Baroque to the present

*Terry Riley (b. 1935)
    tape music, chamber works
    string quartets, orchestral works,
    piano concerto, dramatic works

American composer and performer; the founder of minimalism with his 1964 work, *In C*; interested in electronic and tape music; interested in ethnic music

La Monte Young (b. 1935)
    theatrical and mixed-media
    works, chamber works, vocal
    and electronic works

American composer; used a variety of experimental ideas (some vulgar); was influenced by minimalism and ethnic music; he continues to experiment with time in his music, some pieces having no end yet

Arvo Pärt (b. 1935)
    choral and orchestral works,
    chamber music, piano works

Estonian composer; assimilates older styles with a newly created modern tonality

Steve Reich (b. 1936)
    tape and electronic works,
    orchestral works, chamber music,
    writings

American composer and percussionist; one of the innovators of minimalism

Olly Wilson (b. 1937)
    orchestral and vocal works,
    electronic works, chamber music

African-American composer, teacher, and writer; interested in electronic and African music

*Philip Glass (b. 1937)
    dramatic works, orchestral and
    vocal works, piano works

American composer and performer; one of the innovators of minimalism

David Del Tredici (b. 1937)
    songs, orchestral works, vocal
    and piano works, choral music

American; known as the father of neo-romanticism; influenced by literature

Charles Wuorinen (b. 1938)
    symphonies, concertos, other
    orchestral works, chamber music,
    vocal and choral works, writings

American composer, pianist, and teacher; continued use of serialism

Joan Tower (b. 1938)
    orchestral works, concertos,
    chamber music, fanfares

American composer and pianist; mainstream composer influenced by Beethoven and Stravinsky

*John Corigliano (b. 1938)
    film scores, opera, orchestral
    works, symphonies, vocal works,
    electronic music, band music,
    chamber music, choral music

American composer; addresses important social issues in his sometimes intense music; one of our composers to watch for future generations

Barbara Kolb (b. 1939)
    orchestral works, chamber music,
    vocal works, tape music

American composer; known for her
serialism and pointillism; first American
woman to win the Prix de Rome

*Ellen Taaffe Zwilich (b. 1939)
    orchestral works, concertos,
    chamber music, symphonies,
    choral music, vocal works

American composer and violinist; very
popular, busy, and noteworthy composer

Brian Ferneyhough (b. 1943)
    orchestral, chamber, vocal,
    piano and electroacoustic works

British composer and teacher

Tania Justina León (b. 1943)
    stage works, orchestral and vocal
    works, chamber music, electronic
    works

Cuban-American composer and pianist of
mixed descent; influenced by gospel, jazz,
African, and Cuban elements

*Paul Lansky (b. 1944)
    chamber music, electronic and
    computer music including an
    electronic opera

American pioneer in digital sound
synthesis

Laurie Anderson (b. 1947)
    works of non-traditional genre

American performance artist and
composer; also a painter and teacher

*John Adams (b. 1947)
    operas, orchestral and vocal
    works, chamber music, piano
    works, band music

American composer and conductor;
expanded the new language of
minimalism and neo-romanticism

*Andrew Lloyd Webber (b. 1948)
    stage works, choral-orchestral
    works, film scores

British composer of extraordinary
contemporary fame and success

Libby Larsen (b. 1950)
    stage works, electronic works,
    orchestral and vocal works,
    chamber music

American composer

John Zorn (b. 1953)
    film and TV scores, instrumental
    works

American composer; uses a Kaleidoscopic
approach to composition

Danny Elfman (b. 1953)
    film scores

American film-score composer

Tobias Picker (b. 1954)
    operas, chamber music,
    concertos, piano and vocal
    works

American composer; especially important for his operas

Tan Dun (b. 1957)
    film scores, orchestral works,
    operas, vocal works

Chinese composer and conductor; he strives to create multicultural, multimedia programs that obscure the boundaries between classical and non-classical, East and West, avant-garde and indigenous art forms[5]

Hanns Zimmer (b. 1957)
    film scores

German-born composer; innovator in the use of computer-synthesized soundtracks combined with orchestral music

Uematsu Nobuo (b. 1959)
    videogame scores

Japanese composer of videogame music (*Final Fantasy Series*); he is changing the perception of art music among our youth

Coda: Once again, this representation of composers here is limited due to the vast number of working composers today. The website, http://www.composers21.com/? is a significant attempt to create a database of living composers.

---

[5] http://www.schirmer.com/composers/tan_bio.html

Chapter 3

ℭℜ

Genres[1]

This section is a list of common genres one will encounter in the study of music. Definitions are presented for each genre as they emerged in music history. If the genre experienced significant changes throughout multiple eras, then the changes are noted in each musical period.

Antiquity

We know that the musicians in Antiquity performed songs (a singer with an instrumental accompaniment), choruses, and instrumental pieces. We also have accounts of large instrumental ensembles, but we are unclear as to what music they performed. There were many competitions and virtuosity was important in performance. The majority of the surviving fragments are dramatic songs. Musicians developed songs for specific social functions including funerals, battles, weddings, etc. Intellectuals who wrote about music warned the public not to mix genres of song with inappropriate functions.[2] (For instance, a battle song at a wedding would be inappropriate.)

1. Hymn
Our earliest surviving hymns were monophonic songs of praise in the Christian church. St. Ambrose (340-97) is credited with some of the earliest uses of the hymn.

2. Incidental music
Music that is used in connection with a play is called incidental music. The music may be played or sung before an act, between acts, or during acts. As long as there have been plays, there has been incidental music.

3. Song
A song is a form of musical expression in which the human voice is the primary focus, usually presenting a poetic text. Typically, a song is short and simple in form. Songs existed in every musical time period and their history is particular to each period.

---

[1]For complete descriptions of genres, consult *The New Harvard Dictionary of Music* or, for more detailed explanations, the individual articles concerning each genre in *The New Grove Dictionary of Music and Musicians*.
[2]Bonds, p. 4.

The Middle Ages

Vocal genres became numerous in the Middle Ages. Many genres consisted of single melodies, while others showed the development of polyphony in the middle of the era.

4. Alba
An alba was a type of song of the troubadours and trouvères [see below, numbers 38 and 39] that portrayed the parting of two lovers (usually involved in an illicit affair) who are awakened in the morning by a watchman or friend.

5. Antiphon
An antiphon was a type of liturgical chant that was usually presented in conjunction with a Psalm. Many of the antiphons used the same melody with different words. Originally, they were intended to be sung by a group.

6. Ballade
A ballade is one of the three fixed forms (*formes fixes*) that were popular in French poetry and music in the 14ᵗʰ and 15ᵗʰ centuries. Usually, the musical composition contained three stanzas of seven or eight lines each. The stanzas shared a refrain of one or two lines. Ballades existed in both monophonic and polyphonic textures.

7. Ballata
A ballata is an Italian poetic and musical form that emerged in the mid 1200s and was cultivated into the 1400s. As a musical piece in the 1300s (during the Ars Nova), it was usually polyphonic and secular.

8. Caccia
A caccia (hunt or chase) was a lively secular Italian poetic and musical work from the 14ᵗʰ and 15ᵗʰ centuries. The texts dealt with some sort of hunting or chase, were often in a canon, and were sometimes noisy with shouts and cries.

9. Canon
A canon is the imitation of a complete theme by one or more voices at the same pitch as the primary statement. There are many types of canons and the history of the genre is lengthy. Canons have been composed in every musical era.

10. Canso (canzo)
A canso is a type of troubadour song whose topic focuses on love.

11. Chanson
A chanson was a French song. This genre has a lengthy history beyond the Middle Ages. The term could refer to a number of types of song including those sung by the troubadours and trouvères.[3]

---

[3]See the article, "Chanson" in *The New Harvard Dictionary of Music*, edited by Don Randel.

12. Chant

A chant is plainsong. It is a single melody, performed in free rhythm, often associated with religious ceremonies. There were several dialects of chant, the most common of which today is the Roman style, reorganized in the 6th century as *Gregorian chant*.

13. Clausula

Originally, the term *clausula* meant *cadence*. Then, in the Notre Dame repertoire of the 12th and 13th centuries, a clausula was a passage of liturgical polyphony in discant style on a melismatic fragment from one of the responsorial chants.

14. Conductus

A conductus was a medieval song for one or more voices. It was most often serious in nature or even sacred, and used a rhythmical Latin verse.

15. Gradual

A gradual was a sung chant from the Proper of the Mass. It was sung as responsorial psalmody, (one verse was sung by a soloist, and the verse was then completed or repeated by the choir).

16. Hocket

Hockets were pieces that utilized the hocket technique. The hocket technique was made popular in polyphonic music of the Ars Nova and the Trecento. It was characterized by the distribution of a melodic line between two voices in such a way so that one voice rested while the other voice performed the "missing" pitches. The voices were continually overlapping and interrupting one another.

17. Hymn

See above, number 1.

18. Incidental music

See above, number 2.

19. Lauda

A lauda was a non-liturgical, monophonic, religious song with texts most often in Italian. They were usually vigorous and popular in nature.

20. Lai

A lai was a type of French lyric poetry whose form was long and irregular. It probably originated around 1200 and was sung by the troubadours and trouvères.

21. Lied

German polyphonic Lieder were usually arrangements of folk or popular songs, originally for two to four voices. The tune was usually in the treble and the piece was often homorhythmic.

22. Madrigal (this is the *Medieval* madrigal)

Madrigals from 14th-century Italy were poetic and musical forms that were not related to the later Renaissance genre of the same name. These early madrigals usually consisted of two or three stanzas of three lines of text each, followed by two lines of text called a ritornello. Most of these madrigals were set polyphonically for two voices.

23. Mass

The Mass is the most important service in the Catholic liturgy. As a genre, a Mass implies a setting of the ordinary texts of the Mass (*Kyrie, Gloria, Credo, Sanctus,* and *Agnus Dei)* as a unified musical work. This sort of musical composition (a setting of the five texts as a whole) for the Mass service was not created until the 14th century. Our most notable, early, surviving example of this polyphonic cycle, is Machaut's, *Messe de Notre Dame* (*Mass of Notre Dame*) from the 1360s. We believe that soloists sung these Masses until the late 1400s.

24. Meistergesang (and Minnesang)

A Meistergesang was a song that Meistersingers sung. Our sources are few and it appears that these songs were often transmitted orally. The traditions of the German Minnesinger (and the singing of their songs known as *Minnesang* or *Minnelieder*) date back to the time period between 1150 and 1325. The Meistersingers (those who performed Meistergesang) perpetuated this German tradition and continued it into the late Renaissance. In fact, one could still find guilds as late as the early 19th century.

25. Minnesang

See above, number 24.

26. Minstrel song

Before 1300, the term minstrel could be applied to a variety of professional entertainers. Of those entertainers, musicians gained status as the centuries progressed, so much so, that guilds were formed to promote their education and profession. It appears that most documents refer to these minstrels as instrumentalists only, meaning that the minstrel songs were either songs that they accompanied or songs that they performed alone on an instrument.

27. Morality play

A morality play was a Medieval drama with music that was intended to teach moral values of some sort. Hildegard wrote the first one.

28. Motet

Motets in the 13th century began as sacred, polyphonic works for two or three voices. The motet was created when a text was added to an existing clausula [See above, number 13]. The texts could be French or Latin, or even, have two texts. The early motets used the rhythmic modes and the lower voice was often based on chant.

By the 14th century, motets lost their association with chant, were newly composed, and were more secular than sacred. We believe that soloists performed Medieval motets.

29. Musical play

Musical plays of the 13th century were built around narrative, pastoral songs called *pastourelles* [See below, number 31]. These plays could contain monophonic or polyphonic songs. The most famous secular musical play is Adam de la Halle's *Jeu de Robin et de Marion* (ca. 1284).

30. Organum

Organum is the first type of polyphony about which we know. This early organum, called *parallel organum*, consisted of a chant to which a second, newly composed, voice (the organal voice) was added. At first, the added voice moved in parallel motion with the chant, creating mostly intervals of fourths, fifths, and octaves. Later, organum displayed a more ornate top voice set against the slower (now augmented) chant voice. This type was called *organum purum*.

Near the end of the 12th century, in Paris, at Notre Dame in particular, rhythmic modes were applied to the voices creating a new, modern rhythmic polyphony. This new *discant organum* could contain two, three, or four polyphonic voices.

31. Pastourelle

A pastourelle was a strophic genre of song used by the troubadours and the trouvères. The texts of these songs were in the nature of a dialogue between a shepherdess and a knight who was trying to seduce her. The shepherdess was usually portrayed as more clever than the knight who escaped his escapades through her own invention or, more commonly, through a rescue by other shepherdesses or her family. These songs survive in various languages including, Old Provençal, Old French, Medieval Latin, Iberian, and German.

32. Plainchant (plainsong)

See above, number 12.

33. Rondeau

In the early 14th century, poetic forms of rondeaux [that's the plural of rondeau] were often set polyphonically for three or four voices. The rondeau was one of the three French *formes fixes* (fixed poetic forms), and followed the pattern, ABaAabAB (with the capital letters indicating a refrain).

34. Rondellus

In England in the 13th century, a rondellus was a genre based on a compositional technique called *voice exchange* (*Stimmtausch*, in German). Musical material was exchanged between voices, while, on occasion, the bottom voice could be an independent part made up of a repeated phrase. If all of the voice parts participated in the exchange, it might look like the following arrangement of exchanged musical sections. Note that all of the musical sections had to work together in the harmonic texture.

Voice 1	A	B	C
Voice 2	B	C	A
Voice 3	C	A	B

35. Saltarello

We only have four surviving saltarellos from the 1300s. A saltarello was a cheerful, sprightly Italian dance. Typically, the pieces were instrumental works. These dances continued to be popular throughout the musical periods into the 19th century. Saltarellos became known as *jumping dances*, characterized by triplets in 4/4 meter.

36. Sequence

Sequences first appeared in the 9th century and continued to be used until the early Renaissance. A sequence was a chant (usually elaborate) that was part of the official liturgy of the Catholic Church. Typically, it was sung in the Mass after the *Alleluia*.

37. Trope

A trope was a chant that was part of the liturgy consisting of newly composed words, music, or both. New words or music were added to this pre-existing chant. Tropes were usually more elaborate pieces.

38. Troubadour song

Troubadours were composer-poets from southern France who flourished from the 1100s through the 1200s. Their song texts were in the Old Provençal language (sometimes called Occitan) and focused on love and political or moral issues.[4]

39. Trouvère song

Trouvères were composer-poets in northern France who were called the "inventors of song." Their song texts also dealt with love, but were written in old Medieval French.[5]

40. Virelai

A virelai was one of the three French *formes fixes* (fixed forms) of poetry prominent in the 14th and 15th centuries. The outline of the structure was AbbaA (with the capital letters indicating the refrain).

The Renaissance

Instrumental music began to be more widespread as new keyboard genres developed. Vocal music was popular in both the sacred and secular arenas.

41. Air

An air is a tune that can be vocal or instrumental. In the 16th century, the term (also Ayre) was usually applied to vocal tunes. The term was also used later in opera to distinguish it from an aria or recitative. In this case, and in French opera in particular, the term *air* implied a more declamatory style rather than the typical bel canto Italian aria.

---

[4]We have about 2,600 troubadour poems and 260 of their melodies.
[5]We have about 2,130 of their poems and 1400 melodies.

42. Allemande

Allemandes began as Renaissance dances that were popularized as independent instrumental pieces from around 1580 to the end of the Baroque in 1750. They became standard dances that were used as one of the four dances in solo suites.

43. Anthem

An anthem is an English choral composition usually of religious or moral nature that was performed in a ceremonial context. In Protestant churches, the anthem was the counterpart to the Catholic motet. (See Baroque and Classic)

44. Ballade

See above, number 6.

45. Ballet

There is a complex history of dance in association with music. As a genre, we usually think of the ballet developing in the late Renaissance. Catherine de'Medici helped to create the elevated art form by commissioning works that unified music, poetry, and dance with a single dramatic plot. One of the first ballets of these sorts was the *Ballet comique de la Reine* from 1581 whose music was composed by Lambert de Beaulieu and Jacques Salmon. Ballet, as we think of it today, began to flourish under Louis XIV who was an expert dancer and advocate of the art.

46. Branle

A branle was a 15th century English dance step (brawl). In the 16th century, the branle was a French dance for a group of people and based on a side step while the group held hands.

47. Canzona

A canzona was an instrumental composition popular in the 16th and 17th centuries that modeled itself after the homorhythmic French vocal chanson. These were popular through the Baroque.

48. Chanson

See above, number 11. In the Renaissance, a chanson was likely a French, homorhythmic, or an imitative polyphonic, four-part vocal work.

49. Chorale

Chorales first appeared in the middle of the 16th century as congregational songs (or hymns) of the German Protestant Church. Martin Luther is credited with the most significant contribution to the early repertoire, drawing his texts for his 34 chorales from the Psalms.

50. Fauxbourdon

Fauxbourdon was a 15th century technique of composing. A fauxbourdon consisted of a pre-existing chant under which a lower voice in parallel sixths was composed. A third voice was then improvised a fourth below the chant. Pieces that used this technique were called fauxbordons.

51. Frottola

Frottole were extraordinarily popular in Italy from the 1490s to the 1530s. They were works for four voices, usually light in character, and were often homorhythmic. Instrumental transcriptions of these vocal works were common.

52. Galliard (gagliarda)

A galliard was a cheerful, boisterous court dance of Italian origin from the 1500s. The meter was usually in 6/8 with hemiolas simulating 3/4 measures.

53. German Polyphonic Lieder

See above, number 21.

54. Hymn

Hymns continued in use and were set polyphonically in the Renaissance.

55. Incidental music

See above, number 2.

56. Intermedio

An intermedio was a piece of either instrumental music, or of either staged or non-staged vocal music that was performed between the acts of a play. These musical entertainments were popular in Ferrara, Italy as early as in the late 1400s. By the end of the Renaissance, these intermedi could be extraordinarily lavish including songs, madrigals, and instrumental pieces for up to 60 singers and 24 instrumentalists.

57. Lied

See above, number 18.

58. Lute song

Songs written for the lute became popular in the Renaissance. The pieces were usually binary, and were polyphonic in that the "accompanying lines" were often melodies themselves.

59. Madrigal (the *Renaissance* type)

Madrigals of the 16th century emerged in the 1520s/30s as a higher art form derived from the earlier, lighter, popular, Italian frottola. These madrigals were originally set polyphonically and/or homorhythmically for four voices to a text consisting of one stanza of poetry in a free rhyme scheme. By 1550, five-voice settings were the norm, giving way in the next decades to settings of experimentation, both texturally and harmonically. By 1580, the madrigal was the most modern sort of composition. By 1600, madrigals with basso continuo parts appeared. By the 1640s, the genre all but disappeared.

60. Madrigal comedy

The label, madrigal comedy, is our modern term for a group of Italian vocal pieces (often madrigals) that were unified in some narrative (telling a story) or descriptive way. These cycles emerged in the 1560s and were especially popular from about 1590 to 1608. They were designed for private musical gatherings and as far as we know, they were not intended as staged productions.

61. March

In the early 1500s, European armies marched to standard drumming patterns. Each army had its own rhythmic pattern as well as other military signals that utilized trumpets or fifes. The modern military band developed in the mid 1600s and by the 1800s, a repertoire for this musical group emerged. A march, then, is a musical work, composed for a band (originally of military association) that could be performed in a military function or apart from it.

62. Masque

Masques were entertainments that involved music, poetry, scenery, costumes, and dancing. They were most popular in England at the end of the Renaissance and during the first few decades of the 1600s. We think of these works today as "semi-operas". There were similar productions in Italy and France. The French productions focused more on dancing.

63. Mass

See above, number 23. Renaissance masses were typically written for three (early on) to six voices. By the late Renaissance, the number of voices varied greatly. Masses were multi-movement polyphonic works for voices alone (a cappella). By the time of Josquin, (late 1400s) choirs were used in performance. Previously, soloists sung the polyphony.

64. Motet

The Renaissance motet typically suggested a Latin, vocal work of religious nature for a cappella choir. The history of this genre is actually complex. [See the article on "Motet" in the 2001, *New Grove Dictionary of Music and Musicians*.]

65. Partita

In the late 1500s and early 1600s a partita was a variation on a traditional melody.

66. Passion

A Passion is a musical work that sets the New Testament account of the crucifixion of Jesus. As a composition, the work was usually performed on Palm Sunday and Good Friday. The Renaissance Passions were polyphonic choral settings. Passion settings continued into the 20th century.

67. Pavane (pavana)

A pavane was an Italian court dance from the 1500s. It is typically slow and processional in nature and in 4/2 or 4/4 meter.

68. Prelude

A prelude typically functioned as an introduction and as an establishment of pitch or tonality to a larger set of pieces.

69. Quodlibet

A quodlibet is a composition in which popular tunes or texts are presented as a mosaic creating humor or displaying technical virtuosity. The term was first applied to music in 1544 and the genre reached its popularity in the 18th century.

70. Requiem

A Requiem is a Mass written for a person who has died. The Latin Requiem Mass was standardized in 1570 and Renaissance composers set Requiem Masses as musical works.

71. Ricercar (ricercare, plural)

A ricercar was an instrumental piece that often had an introductory purpose. The earliest types were homophonic and appeared in lute manuscripts from the early Renaissance. Other ricercare were composed for organ shortly thereafter. The polyphonic ricercar was more popular in the late Renaissance and into the Baroque. Solo lutes and keyboards tended to be the primary forces, but there were several ensemble ricercare published as well, disappearing by 1632, and being replaced by the keyboard type.

72. Toccata

Toccatas first appeared in sets of lute dances in 1536. See below, number 122.

73. Verset

A verset was a short piece for organ that was intended to replace a verse of chant in the liturgy. Typically, the organist would play the odd-numbered verses while the choir sang the even-numbered ones. Much of the time these pieces were improvised, but composers did write them down for use in the service. This tradition extended from around 1400 to the early 20th century.

74. Villancico

A villancico was a Spanish form of poetry with a particular rhyme scheme and order. Polyphonic settings of these poems have created a vast repertory of Spanish song.

The Baroque

Instrumental genres began to take a primary position next to opera. Sacred music was still widespread. Basso continuo developed, creating a new texture available in music performance: homophony. Basso continuo is not a genre, but it is used in almost every Baroque genre.

Basso Continuo Explained

Basso Continuo means a "continuous bass". Basso continuo served as the bass line in music from the 17th and 18th centuries. This bass line consisted of an instrument capable of playing chords (organ, harpsichord, lute, etc.) and at least one melody instrument capable of sustaining a bass line (viol, bassoon, cello [today], etc.). Both instruments saw only the bass line when performing. The keyboard (or chordal instrument) was expected to "realize" the figured bass—that is, to fill in the chords at sight as a form of improvisation, viewing the written symbols below or above the bass line. Thus, there was an accompaniment of chords that served as the harmonic foundation for the homophony or polyphony above it in other parts. This basso continuo part was also call the figured bass. (Figured bass is also called thoroughbass.) The players who performed this basso continuo line were called the basso continuo group. (It takes at least two players, and the composer can add extra players to the group if desired. Monteverdi preferred large continuo groups.)

— Emilio de' Cavalieri's *Rappresentazione di Anima e di Corpo* (1600) was the first publication to feature a figured bass.

---

75. Allemande
See above, number 42.

76. Anthem
The English anthem in the Baroque utilized the new musical style of basso continuo with solo and choral voices and instruments with instrumental passages.

77. Aria
An aria is a self-contained piece for solo voice, accompanied by instruments. An aria often exists within a larger genre, such as in an opera, oratorio, or cantata.

The aria of the late Baroque was the cornerstone of operas, cantatas, and oratorios. It was a solo work for a singer and orchestral ensemble of virtually any size. Several aria forms developed during this time and the da capo form, in particular, reached its height. By the late Baroque, arias were considered the character's emotional display, and were often paired with a recitative of more narrative nature.

78. Ballad opera
A ballad opera was an English genre in which spoken dialogue alternated with songs consisting of new words that were set to traditional or popular tunes. The first and most famous of this sort is John Gay's *The Beggar's Opera* from 1728.

79. Ballet
Ballets continued their success focusing on simple, sung tunes, instrumental pieces, and dances. In the Late Baroque, ballets began to loose their sung pieces and were confined mostly to instrumental pieces and dances.

80. Bourrée

This popular Baroque dance form was lively, in duple meter, and in binary form. It was danced at the court of Louis XIV and in Lully's operas. It could also serve as an independent instrumental piece.

81. Cantata

In the 17th century, an Italian cantata was a vocal work for a soloist and basso continuo. Cantatas up until the 1630s contained simple arias, strophic variations, and passages of monody. This early type of cantata was usually a small-scale work intended for more private social gatherings. It was originally secular.

In the middle Baroque, the cantata became very popular. The texts were usually divided into recitative and aria sections. The arias began to expand in size and importance, mirroring stylistic changes in opera arias at the time. The cantata still had secular associations and could be for one or more soloists.

The Italian cantata of the early 18th century still looked like the cantata of the earlier Baroque except that now the forms of the arias were commonly da capo. The Lutheran cantata (which had actually developed in the 1600s) became longer and frequently employed soloists and choirs. These Lutheran cantatas were a combination of recitative/aria sets, choruses, and chorales on German sacred or moral texts.

82. Canzona

See above, number 47.

83. Chaconne

The chaconne was a Baroque form (similar to the passacaglia) that was a continuous variation based on a chord progression. In 1627 Frescobaldi published the first such variations for keyboard in *Partite sopra ciaconna*.

By the late Baroque, instrumental chaconnes were popular in England, Austria, and Germany. Around 1750, the genre began to fall out of favor.

84. Choral fugue

Fugues written for choirs emerged in the Baroque. They continued to thrive in sacred music through the 19th century.

85. Chorale

See above, number 49. The typical Baroque chorale was usually homophonic and homorhythmic, and its several stanzas of text were set strophically.

86. Chorale prelude (organ chorale)

A chorale prelude was a composition for organ that was based on a German Protestant chorale tune. It often served as an introduction to the singing of the chorale on which it was based. An *organ chorale* implied a more elaborate work for organ (often polyphonic and sectional) based on the chorale tune. It could serve as an independent piece apart from the singing of the chorale.

87. Concerto

In the early Baroque, a concerto was a work for a diverse ensemble of voices or instruments, or a combination of the two. The term meant to *concert*, or to *unite* and *join together*. Typically, in the early and Middle Baroque, concertos were sacred works for voices and instruments. **Grand concertos** were large-scale sacred works for soloists, chorus, and instrumental accompaniment. These grand concertos were performed at St. Mark's Cathedral in Venice. This polychoral style became known as the Venetian style, or music from the Venetian School. **Sacred concertos** were vocal compositions on a sacred text for one or more soloists with instrumental accompaniment. They, too, could include a chorus such as in a grand concerto, creating a confusing similarity.

By the late Baroque, a concerto usually implied an instrumental group that used some sort of *concertante* principle, (that of alternating, or contending, one section of the group with the other). There were three types of concertos in the late Baroque. Each was a multi-movement (usually three movements) composition for strings, basso continuo, and occasionally winds. Most concertos used some sort of ritornello form. See Chapter 4, *Forms*, number 4.

a. Concerto grosso

A concerto grosso used a small group of soloists that opposed (alternated with) a large tutti group. The smaller ensemble was called the concertino and the large group was called the ripieno. The basso continuo played with both groups.

b. Solo concerto

A solo concerto was organized similarly to the concerto grosso except that the solo group was only one soloist with the basso continuo, rather than several. A cadenza, an improvised solo by the main soloist, was often inserted near the ends of the movements. The basso continuo did not play in the cadenzas.

c. Ripieno concerto

A ripieno concerto utilized no alternation between groups of any size. It used the tutti (ripieno) all the way through the piece. (Yes, this was similar to a sinfonia). See below, number 118.

88. Courante

A courante was a Baroque dance in triple meter that eventually was a regular movement of the suite. There were Italian, English, and French types.

89. Fantasia

A fantasia was an instrumental work that was characterized by imaginative, and sometimes exaggerated, figures in an attempt to give the feeling of improvisation. It was free in form and could serve an introductory function, such as to a fugue.

90. French Ouverture

A French ouverture was a two-part form (slow with dotted rhythms, then fast and often fugal) usually for orchestral ensemble. The slow section could return at the end of the fast section, creating a ternary or rounded binary structure. These ouvertures often were placed as the first movement in a suite.

91. Fugue

The fugue was the most highly developed type of imitative counterpoint. A fugue is a form and a genre. Fugues could be written for keyboards, instrumentalists, or vocal groups. See Chapter 4, *Forms*, number 7.

92. Gigue (English, *jig*)

A gigue was a fast Baroque dance that was usually the last movement in a suite. It was in binary form and in a compound meter of 6/8 or 12/8.

93. Grand concerto

See above, number 87.

94. Hymn

There is a long history of hymnody, including the various types of American, Lutheran, English, etc. hymns. By the 18th century, hymns were often compositions of choral homophony.

95. Incidental music

See above, number 2.

96. Intermezzo

In the 18th century an intermezzo was a comic, theatrical, musical scene that was performed between the acts of a serious opera. These scenes were eventually removed from the larger opera and performed on their own as two-act comic operas called, intermezzi.

97. Ländler

A Ländler was an Austrian dance in slow 3/4 time that originated as a folk dance and that later in the 18th century, became a popular ballroom dance. It remained popular into the early 19th century.

98. Masque

A Masque was a theatrical entertainment in England popular from 1601 to the 1630s. The performance involved costumes, scenery, dancing, music, and poetry. The works were not complete operatic compositions, but rather collections of poetry and music. Consequently, a complete masque does not survive, only portions.

99. Mass

See above, numbers 23 and 63. In the 18th and 19th centuries, masses continued to flourish. The individual musical divisions now could include arias, recitatives, and choruses. An orchestral ensemble of some sort, including in the Baroque, the basso continuo group, usually accompanied the voices.

100. Minuet

A minuet was an elegant dance in 3/4 meter that experienced special popularity from 1650 to 1800, appearing first in France. It was usually in binary form with symmetrical phrasing and strong emphases on the first beats of each measure.

101. Motet
Motets in the Baroque were choral or solo works with instrumental accompaniment (basso continuo at least). Texts could be in German, Italian or Latin and, if for soloist, were arranged in sets of arias and recitatives. We have many surviving examples of solo motets. See below, number 137.

102. Opera
The Florentine Camerata (a group of intellectuals in Florence) were interested in trying to recreate Greek drama. They mistakeningly thought that Greek plays were sung all the way through. Thus, when they made attempts to imitate the Classic Greek models, opera resulted.

An opera is a drama that is sung throughout, accompanied by instruments and theatrically staged. Jacopo Peri wrote the first opera, *Dafne*, in 1597. It was produced twice in Florence during the carnival season in 1598. The score is not extant. Three of the very first surviving operas include: 1. *Rappresentazione di Anima e di Corpo* ("The Representation of the Soul and the Body") by Emilio de' Cavalieri, produced in Rome, February 1600; 2. *Euridice* by Giulio Caccini, published in January 1601, but not produced in its entirety until December 1602, and 3. *Euridice* by Peri, produced in Florence, October 1601. The most famous early opera is *L' Orfeo* (actually, *La Favola d'Orfeo,* or "The Fable of Orfeo") by Claudio Monteverdi, produced in Mantua in 1607. *Orfeo* is often cited as the first opera or even as the first published opera, but it is not. However, the work is certainly the most famous early opera.

103. Organ chorale
See above, number 86.

104. Oratorio
An oratorio was an extended musical drama with a religious subject that was not staged. This meant that there were no costumes, scenery, or actions. Many oratorios had a narrative thread that took the place of visual display. Originally, oratorios were set to Italian texts. Later, Handel created the English oratorio, the most famous of which is, today, *Messiah* (1742).

105. Ordre
See below, number 122.

106. Organ prelude
German organ preludes of the 17th century were works for organ that often began in a free compositional style and ended in a fugal section.

107. Overture
An overture was a composition for orchestra that was intended as an introductory number for an opera, ballet, or other dramatic genre. In the Baroque, these overtures were usually called *sinfonia* and were in three movements: fast, slow, fast. See below, number 118.

108. Partita

In the early 1700s a partita was another term for a suite. See below, number 122.

109. Passacaglia

A passacaglia was a piece in the Baroque passacaglia form. See Chapter 4, *Forms*, number 11.

110. Passion

See above, number 66. In the Baroque, Passions were composed as multi-movement works containing arias, recitatives, and choruses.

111. Prelude

See above, number 68. By the late Baroque, preludes were often introductory pieces for fugues.

112. Quodlibet

See above, number 69.

113. Recitative

A recitative is a section of music that has been set in a style that imitates and emphasizes the natural accents, rhythms, and flow of speech. Recitative was through-composed with little or no repetition of text. The tempo was typically freer with use of rubato. Early recitative was set for a solo singer with basso continuo and appeared in the early operas, cantatas, oratorios, solo motets, and other dramatic works of 1600 and the years following. Recitative passages could be monologues, or dialogues between two or more characters. This sort of text setting began in Italy and spread to Germany, France, and England. Recitative was valued for its expressive quality. This new expressive setting was so popular that one finds the score marking, "stile recitativo" indicating for performers to sing or play in this manner. There were two types of recitative by the end of the 17th century.

> 1. ***Recitativo secco*** (simple, or dry recitative, also *recitativo semplice*)
> Secco recitative involved only the singer and the basso continuo group.

> 2. ***Recitativo accompagnato*** (accompanied, also *stromentato* [with instruments], or *recitativo obbligato*)
> Accompanied recitative involved the singer and the basso continuo group, but also other instruments from the orchestral ensemble. This recitative was more dramatic in nature and was often reserved for moments of intensity or importance.

By the late Baroque, recitative was no longer the emotional focus of dramatic works. In operas of the 18th century, the recitatives were considered necessary evils to the drama in that they were the passages in which the plots advanced and the actions took place. Some composers even hired out the composition of their recitatives. (The arias were the emotional focal points by 1700.)

114. Ricercar (ricercare)

See above, number 71.

115. Sacred concerto

See above, number 87.

116. Sarabande

A sarabande is a slow Baroque dance movement in triple meter, characterized by an accented dotted note on the second beat of each measure. Its form was usually binary with regular four or eight measure phrasing.

117. Serenata

A serenata was a long and elaborate cantata that was composed to celebrate a special occasion or civic event. They were dramatic in nature and usually performed outdoors in the evening. Most composers in the middle of the 18th century composed serenatas. Serenatas were performed with costumes and scenery, but usually no stage action.

118. Sinfonia

See above, number 106. The term sinfonia was used for several distinctions in the late Baroque and early Classic periods. The term could denote a symphony, sonata, canzona, *sonata da chiesa*, or a keyboard or instrumental ensemble that was a prelude to a Mass, motet, or set of dances. By the mid-18th century, the term commonly referred to an overture of an Italian opera.

119. Sonata

The common use of the term **sonata** denotes a genre for a solo instrument and keyboard accompaniment (or the basso continuo group in the Baroque). Sonatas were considered chamber music and typically were composed in three or four movements. Keyboard sonatas were written for the keyboard alone (harpsichord, or much later, piano). The history of the sonata and the term's usage is complex.[6]

120. Sonata da camera

The *sonata da camera* (sonata for the chamber) was a court sonata particular to the years 1650 to 1740 that was written for one or more melody instruments and basso continuo. It was associated with dance in its earliest forms. By the 18th century it was a work in three movements: fast, slow, fast.

121. Sonata da chiesa (sonata for the church)

The *sonata da chiesa* (sonata for the church) was a chamber work for instrumental ensemble (most often one or more melody instruments and basso continuo) popular from the 1650s to the 1770s. It was typically a multi-movement work, often beginning with a slow movement, of contrasting sections. It is distinguished from the *sonata da camera* by its serious nature and use of counterpoint. Additionally, the organ was specified often as the continuo instrument.

---

[6]See *The New Harvard Dictionary of Music*, pages 760-63.

122. Suite

A suite, also called *partita* or *ordre*, was a multi-movement instrumental composition made up of a series of short, contrasting dance movements. The number and type of movements varied greatly throughout much of the suite's popularity. German suites from the mid-Baroque showed a consistent organization of four movements consisting of an Allemande, Courante, Sarabande, and Gigue. Suites of all sorts (including for keyboard alone) were very popular into the 19th century.

123. Toccata

See Renaissance. As a Baroque genre, a toccata was a virtuosic composition for keyboard or plucked stringed instruments that exhibited characteristics similar to improvisation. The pieces did not utilize counterpoint, but rather were displays of brilliant passage-work and impressive figurations.

124. Tragédie lyrique

Tragédie lyrique was a type of French serious opera often associated with the operas of Lully. The genre usually contained five acts preceded by a prologue, drawing its subject from Greek mythology or courtly romance.

The Classic Period

Instrumental genres, for the first time in history, began their rise to dominance that seemed to take its strongest root around 1810.

125. Allemande

See above, number 42.

126. Anthem

William Billings (1746-1800) and Lowell Mason (1792-1872) supplied anthems for American churches. The tradition continued into the 19th and 20th centuries as a choral-orchestral work with religious associations with English text.

127. Aria

See above, number 77. Additionally, arias in the classic era were composed in ternary or rondo form to reflect more modern tastes. Also, concert arias were composed and performed apart from the larger genres.

128. Ballet

See above, number 79.

129. Concerto

By the classic period, of the three types of Baroque concertos, only solo types remained popular.

130. Divertimento

The term divertimento was applied to lighter, instrumental, entertainment music or music that was intended for a specific occasion. These pieces were usually multi-movement works for a small to medium-sized chamber group of players.

131. Incidental music

See above, number 2.

132. Intermezzi

See above, number 96.

133. Ländler

See above, number 97.

134. Lied

A German poem that was usually lyric and strophic was set to music as a Lied (German song) for a solo singer and a keyboard. The musical settings in the late 18th century were numerous, but for the most part unremarkable. See below, number 164.

135. March

In the 18th and 19th centuries, marches were commonly found in operas and ballets. They were also composed as separate pieces for either dancing purposes or as stylized works for the concert hall. Nineteenth-century composers especially favored funeral marches.

136. Melodrama

Melodramas became in vogue in the 1770s (Mozart was enthralled by their novelty) and continued to thrive up to the present. A melodrama consisted of instrumental music with spoken dialogue. The spoken text could alternate with instrumental music or could be placed on top of it. Considering our films of today, the effects of this 18th century invention on our current culture are striking.

137. Minuet

See above, number 100. Minuets were extremely popular during the late 18th century. Minuets could serve as closing movements of opera overtures and as movements in symphonies and string quartets. The phrase, *tempo di minuetto* implied all of the stylistic attributes of this popular genre without confining the composition at hand to the minuet form. See Chapter 4, *Forms*, number 9.

138. Motet

By the classic era, motets were solo works for a singer and orchestra, structured usually in sets of recitatives and arias, ending with an aria on the text, *Alleluia*.

139. Opera buffa

Opera buffa first developed as an enlightened sort of comic opera in 1760 with Piccinni's *La buona figliuola*. This sort of comic opera could address moral issues and utilized a more complicated cast of characters than earlier comedies such as the intermezzo or the other comedies from the Baroque. Mozart's three opera buffa, *Le nozze di Figaro* (1786), *Don Giovanni* (1787), and *Così fan tutte* (1790) are considered masterpieces in the genre. Opera buffa, like other types of opera, could contain arias, recitatives, ensembles, choruses, and instrumental pieces with or without dancing.

140. Opera seria

Serious operas continued to flourish alongside comic operas in the Classic era. Libretti written by Pietro Metastasio were especially popular. These operas also could contain arias, recitatives, ensembles, choruses, and instrumental pieces with or without dancing.

141. Overture

See above, number 107.

142. Partita

In the Classic period a partita was a multi-movement instrumental work that usually contained a mixture of dance numbers and abstract (non-dance associated) numbers. Since partitas were intended for soloists, the genre was a chamber piece.

143. Pasticcio

A pasticcio is an opera that was assembled by several composers, each making musical contributions.

144. Quodlibet

See above, number 69.

145. Recitative

See above, number 113. As the practice of basso continuo disappeared in the late 18th century, accompanied recitatives were increasingly more popular.

146. Rondo

The rondo actually originated in the earlier French rondeau, but we consider it a Classic genre today. The genre is a musical piece constructed in the form of a rondo. (See Chapter 4, *Forms*, number 13.) Rondos could be composed independently or as a movement in a larger musical work.

147. Serenade

In the Classic period, a serenade was an instrumental work that could either be a large-scale work for orchestra, or a smaller chamber work for a smaller group. Most serenades contained at least three movements (fast, slow, fast) to which marches, minuets, or movements with soloists were added.

148. Singspiel

A Singspiel was a German comic opera that contained spoken dialogue instead of recitative. Most Singspiele (Mozart's were an exception) contained simple, strophic

Lieder and folk tunes. The settings were frequently of humble life, either rural or exotic, and the characters were static in nature. North German Singspiel appeared in 1752 and continued into the 19th century as an important form of German theater.

149. Sonata

See above, number 119.

150. String quartet

A string quartet is a multi-movement chamber work composed for four solo stringed instruments: two violins, a viola, and a cello. The genre emerged as a Classic-style composition that did not rely on the basso continuo to support the musical material. Rather, all four instruments were considered equal, as in a polite dialogue. Although Haydn made some of the most important contributions to the genre, string quartets appeared first composed by Franz Xaver Richter and other Mannheim composers in the 1750s.

151. String trio

A string trio was a three or four-movement composition for a chamber ensemble of solo players consisting of either two violins and a cello, or a violin, viola, and cello.

152. Symphony

A symphony was a three or four-movement work for orchestra that was created by Sammartini in the 1730s and 40s in Milan. Early symphonies were usually in three movements: fast, slow, fast. By the 1770s, the symphonic organization was typically in four movements as follows:

> Movement I: Tonic key, fast tempo, in sonata form (a slow introduction was optional)
> Movement II: Contrasting key, slower tempo, different form (such as ternary, theme and variations, sonatina)
> Movement III: Tonic key, a Minuet and Trio tempo and form
> Movement IV: Tonic key, fast tempo, in sonata, rondo, or sonata-rondo form
> Symphonies experienced a continual popularity into the 20th century. Some

composers chose to compose within the traditional structure of the genre (Brahms for instance), while others made innovations in form and organization (Berlioz, and the 20th century composers).

The Nineteenth Century

Opera was still one of the main cultural attractions, but by the end of the 19th century, it took a secondary position to instrumental music.

153. Anthem

See above, number 126.

154. Aria

Arias of the 19th century continued their associations with larger works such as oratorios and operas and were also produced independently of larger genres. The forms of arias expanded and were often multi-sectional. In the middle of the century, Wagner created arias whose beginnings and endings were not clearly defined but were instead, part of a continuous flow of dramatic content.

155. Ballade (poetic/vocal)

The German ballade was a narrative poem or song that began to flourish at the end of the 18th century and into the 19th century. Its development is similar to that of a Lied.

156. Ballade (instrumental)

A ballade in this sense is a character piece that was popularized by Chopin, Liszt, and Brahms. These are generally, one-movement works for piano that might have a suggestion of a refrain or of a poetic nature.

157. Ballet

By the 19th century, ballets were large-scale multi-movement works that were comprised of individual dance numbers, usually without vocal music or spoken dialogue.

158. Character piece (miniature)

In the 19th century, one-movement, short, lyrical pieces for piano became popular. These pieces often evoked a particular mood or scene, or were used for pedagogical purposes (etudes). Romantic lyric piano pieces were called a variety of names including, but not limited to, fantasia, mazurka, nocturne, prelude, ballade, etude, intermezzo, rhapsody, polonaise, capriccio, march, waltz, etc.

159. Concerto

Solo concertos continued to thrive. The opening ritornello was usually extended so much so that it functioned as a long expository orchestral section. Some textbooks refer to this as a double exposition form, because the concerto appears to have two expositions: one for the orchestra, and one for the soloist.

160. Etude

An etude is a one-movement study piece for a solo player that focuses on one aspect or technical problem of the instrument.

161. Incidental music

See above, number 2.

162. Intermezzo

In the 19th and 20th centuries, an intermezzo was a middle movement or section of a larger work. Its label implied that the intermezzo was lighter in character than the larger work in which it was placed.

An intermezzo was also a character piece for solo piano in the 19th century.

163. Ländler
See above, number 97.

164. Lied
Lieder of the 19th century took on new musical importance as Schubert and the romantics took the emotional and expressive content of the genre to a higher artistic plane. The songs were written for a solo singer and a pianist and were performed in intimate settings for poetic effect. The forms of Lieder varied, but we have many examples of strophic, modified strophic, and through-composed songs. See Chapter 4, *Forms*, numbers 20, 21, and 24.

165. March
See above, number 61 and 135.

166. Mazurka
A mazurka was a polish folk dance in triple meter that was danced by four, eight, or twelve couples. Although the dance dates back to the early Baroque, it experienced its greatest popularity in Europe in the 1830s and 40s as a salon dance and character piece for piano. For example, Chopin, alone, wrote more than 50 mazurkas.

167. Minstrel song
In the 19th century a minstrel was a member of a troupe of comedic entertainers who capitalized on stereotypes (especially those of a racial nature) and presented comic and entertaining shows, singing minstrel songs. By the early 20th century, the popularity of these minstrel shows was replaced by vaudeville and burlesque. The inflammatory nature of the racism involved in this tradition has been the subject of 20th century discussions.

168. Motet
Choral motets in the 19th century were briefly revived through the Cecilian movement. Composers continued to write them, but there is not a list of characteristics that unifies the genre.

169. Music drama
Wagner called his operas, especially the mature ones, music dramas. His notion was that these new, elevated artistic works combined multiple arts including, music, poetry, scenery, acting, lighting, etc. into one collected artwork, or, *Gesamtkunstwerk*.

170. Nocturne
Certain instrumental works, typically for solo piano in the 19th century, were called nocturnes. John Field first used the title in 1812. They were lyrical character pieces.

171. Opera
There were several types of opera in the 19th century. Generally, operas were staged theatrical productions for soloists, vocal ensembles, and an orchestra. Various types include:

a. German romantic opera

The founder of German romantic opera was Carl Maria von Weber with his *Der Freischütz* of 1821. Although this looked like a Singspiel (because of the spoken dialogue, not its comedy) and melodrama, it laid the foundation for Wagner who later became the main advocate of German opera.

b. Italian opera seria

The founder of 19th –century Italian serious opera was Johann Mayr. His operas were built on the opera reforms made during the 1750s and 60s by Jommelli, Traetta, Gluck, and de Majo.

c. Italian comic opera

The master of Italian comic opera was Rossini. He achieved the idea of continuous plot development within a comedy.

d. Grand opera

Grand operas were dramas of French influence and were productions of great and grand spectacle. These operas were full of ballets, machines, crowd scenes, and attracted the most general of audiences.

e. Opéra comique

Opera comique was a French comic opera that used spoken dialogue instead of recitative. (Like the German Singspiel)

f. Opéra bouffe

The founder of opéra bouffe was Offenbach. This French comic genre satirized the government and leadership.

g. French lyric opera

These lyric operas had romantic centered plots. This genre lay somewhere between opéra comique and grand opera.

h. Italian tragic opera

Verdi created an Italian genre of opera that dominated the 19th century and the next. His operas were traditional in that they contained arias, recitatives, ensembles, and choruses.

i.   Opera semiseria

These operas developed in the late 18th century containing a combination of serious and comic elements. Such an opera might have had ornate arias (as in opera seria) and also the ensemble finales of comic operas.

172. Operetta

In the 19th century, operettas developed in France, then Germany, England, and the U.S. An operetta is a popular form of entertainment consisting of spoken dialogue, songs, and dances, exhibiting a lighter form of theater than traditional opera.

173. Orchestral Lied

In the 19ᵗʰ century, German Lieder were composed for solo voice and orchestra. Sometimes the Lieder were grouped into cycles.

174. Overture

In the 19ᵗʰ century, concert overtures were composed apart from any larger work. These overtures, often programmatic in association, were intended to be performed as concert pieces.

175. Piano quartet

A piano quartet is a multi-movement (usually three or four movements) chamber work composed for a piano and three strings, most often a violin, viola, and cello.

176. Piano trio

A piano trio is a multi-movement (usually three or four movements) chamber work composed for a piano, violin, and cello.

177. Prelude

In the 19ᵗʰ century a prelude was a short, lyrical character piece for piano. Also, in the 19ᵗʰ century, a prelude could be an orchestral introduction for a dramatic work.

178. Program symphony

A program symphony is a multi-movement orchestral work in the form of a symphony that is based on a program of a narrative or descriptive nature.

179. Recitative

In the 19ᵗʰ century, the sections of recitative, aria, and arioso began to lose their distinctions. Wagner achieved the greatest blend of these genres when he created his continuous dramatic scenes of what we call, endless melody.

180. Sonata

See above, number 119.

181. Song cycle

In the 19ᵗʰ century, a song cycle was a group of Lieder (or songs) set to poetry, most often by a single poet, and grouped together either by a narrative or subjective thread. These cycles were intended as private entertainment pieces.

182. String Quartet

See above, number 150.

183. String trio

See above, number 151.

184. Symphonic poem (tone poem)

Franz Liszt invented the symphonic poem in 1853 in Weimar, with his *Les Preludes*, as an alternative to the more traditional multi-movement symphony. A symphonic poem is a one-movement orchestral work whose music is often accompanied by (or at least associated with) a program of poetic or narrative nature. Some of the most innovative techniques of the 19th century were accomplished in this genre.

185. Symphony

See above, number 152. As a genre, the symphony in the 19th century was a cultivated traditional concert piece. Many composers' careers were contingent upon their first symphonic productions. As the 19th century progressed, symphonies typically became longer and more expansive in orchestration and form.

186. Tone poem

See above, number 184.

The Twentieth Century

Art music saw all sorts of changes and innovations in the 20th century. Some composers utilized the older genres while other composers created new ones with no name or categorization. Because so much music was untraditional, the new genres remain largely uncategorized today.

*Modern tonality affected all of the following genres.

187. Anthem

See above, number 126.

188. Ballet

The term ballet came to mean "classical ballet" as other types of dance productions were produced throughout the century. Innovations in the history of dance are as complex and interesting as those in music.

189. Canon

Canons achieved a revival of interest in atonal and tonal music in the 20th century. Additionally, canonic techniques were applied to musical elements other than pitch.

190. Cantata

A cantata in the 20th century merely implied some sort of choral/solo/orchestral work.

191. Contrafact

A contrafact is a jazz composition that has its chord progressions taken from a pre-existing work. New music is then composed on top of the chord progressions. Composers did this with George Gershwin's "I Got Rhythm".

192. Fugue

Fugues experienced a rebirth in the 20th century as new timbres enabled composers to experiment with older forms in the modern style.

193. Incidental music
See above, number 2.

194. Masque
See number 98. The English masque was revived by Vaughan Williams and Britten.

195. Musical
A musical was a popular form of musical theater in the 20th century. It was cultivated mostly in England and America. Musicals could contain songs, choruses, dances, spoken dialogue, melodrama, and ensemble numbers.

196. Opera
Operas lessened in popularity as the 20th century progressed. Typically, operas were still staged works that included arias, ensembles, choruses, and instrumental pieces.

197. Orchestral set
Orchestral sets were multi-movement orchestral works that were composed as an alternative to more traditionally named genres.

198. Passion
See above, number 66. In the 20th century, Passions could be multi-movement choral/orchestral works or choral motets.

199. Passacaglia
In the 20th century, composers found a new interest in contrapuntal forms within new modern tonalities. The passacaglia was one such genre that experienced a revival. See Chapter 4, *Forms*, number 11.

200. Sonata
Many 20th century composers composed sonatas of all sorts. The traditional organization was cultivated alongside new structures of the genre. Typically, a 20th century sonata would be composed for a solo instrument and piano, or a piano alone (piano sonata).

201. String quartet
String quartets continued to be popular throughout the 20th century. The traditional group of two violins, a viola, and a cello is still used.

202. Rondo
Rondos were popular in the 20th century as composers found the use of a refrain novel within the new atonality and other modern innovations.

203. Theme and Variations
Variations experienced continued popularity in the 20th century as orchestral and chamber genres.

Chapter 4

ℭℜ

Musical Forms

Form is the organizing principle in music that is based on contrast, variation, and repetition or restatement. There are several standard forms that have developed over the course of music history. If a composition does not show a recognized pattern it can be labeled, "free form".

1. Bar Form

This is a German form (AAB) commonly found in both music and poetry. In German strophic songs, such as in the Meistersinger songs of the Medieval period, bar form was commonplace. The "A" sections are called the *Stollen* and the "B" section is called the *Abgesang*.

A	B
‖: a b a :‖	‖: c d c :‖

2. Binary Form

Binary form indicates a two-part form diagramed as: AB
Sometimes the internal organization of each part (the A and the B) have repetitions or a binary form of its own. For example the larger organized binary form (AB) might be arranged like the following with more detail.

3. Chaccone

A chaccone is a Baroque form that is based on a repeated chord progression or sequence of chords. It is similar to the passacaglia in that variations take place on top of this chordal repetition. (A passacaglia uses an actual bass melody rather than a chord progression.)

4. Concerto form (or Ritornello form)

The first and last movements of most Baroque concertos were composed in ritornello form. The form is based on an alternation of tutti sections (the ritornello with everyone playing) and solo sections (with only one soloist or small group of soloists [the concertino] playing). The ritornello ("the little thing that returns") recurs throughout, unifying the movement thematically. A typical ritornello form from the late Baroque looks like the following. (Abbreviations: Rit=ritornello; S= Solo; I(i)= major and minor tonic; V (v)=major and minor dominant; III=mediant; vi=submediant)

Rit 1	S 1		Rit 2	S 2 (development)	Rit 3
Tutti	Concertists/or soloist		tutti	soloist(s)	tutti
I (i)	I(i) ⟶ V (or vi, III, v)		in new key	new key ⟶	I(i)

S 3	Cadenza	Rit 4	‖
soloist(s)	soloist w/o orchestra	tutti	
I(i) ———————————————⟶			

5. **Da capo aria form**

The da capo aria emerged as the favorite form of arias in the late Baroque. It was a three part form (ABA) that used two stanzas of poetry, one for the A section, and one for the B section.

A section
>   Instrumental ritornello: in the tonic (I)
>   *Stanza 1*, full statement: moving from I to dominant (V)
>   Ritornello: in V
>   *Stanza 1*, 2nd full statement: going from V back to I
>   Ritornello: in I

B section
>   *Stanza 2*, usually stated only once: in a harmonically contrasting key, usually avoiding the tonic. This B section is often in a different tempo or meter. (*Da capo*, "to the head," then appears in the score, indicating that the performers should return to measure 1 of the piece.)

A section
>   The A section is repeated as before, but with added ornamentation and improvisation by the soloist.

6. **Dal segno aria form**

This aria form looks just like the da capo aria except that the repeat of the A section begins with the first statement of stanza one, rather than with the opening instrumental ritornello. At the end of the B section, *dal segno* ("to the sign") is printed for the performers to return to the previous sign that appeared in the A section.

7. **Fugue**

A fugue is a contrapuntal Baroque form that is highly organized in its beginning (exposition). Following the exposition, the rules of musical rhetoric control the subject and answer statements as the piece develops through contrapuntal means.

Be aware, that the composer can choose two or more voices to create his fugue and can have them enter in any order. For the sake of diagramming, I have chosen four voices, entering from the treble down to the bass. A fugue can be sung or played. Keyboard fugues were very popular, and in this case, the voices are laid out on the keyboard as they would be in the playing of a hymn—roughly, two voices in the right hand, and two voices in the left hand. The main theme is called the *subject*, followed by a version of itself in the dominant, called the *answer*. The exposition of a fugue looks like this:

Exposition:			
Voice I	Subject (tonic)	Countersubject I	Countersubject II	_____
Voice II	_____	Answer (dominant)	Countersubject I	Countersubject II
Voice III	_____	_____	Subject (tonic)	Countersubject I
Voice IV	_____	_____	_____	Answer (dominant)

The fourth voice/instrument to enter rarely gets to state the countersubjects. Following the exposition, the piece becomes complex with statements and answers.

8. **Ground bass form**

A ground bass is a repeating melody, usually placed in the bass. A piece can be organized with this repeating melody as the basis of its formal structure.

9. **Minuet and Trio**

This form is an elegant Baroque dance movement in triple meter, popular especially between 1650 and 1800. A Baroque minuet and trio typically look like the following:

Minuet	Trio	Minuet
A	B	A
a a b b	c c d d	a b

10. **Modified strophic form**

This form is a type of strophic form in which the music varies to some degree in the setting of each stanza of text. Harmonies, keys, and texture can change, but the music remains recognizably the same in each musical repetition.

11. **Passacaglia**

A passacaglia is a Baroque form that is based on a short, repeated bass-line melody that serves as the foundation for continuous variations in the upper voices. The piece is usually in a rather slow triple meter.

12. **Ritornello form** (see *Concerto form*)

13. **Rondo form**

A typical rondo form from the eighteenth century is designed thusly: ABACA.
The rondo originated in the French rondeau of the Baroque. Since then, variations of the form have appeared. The rondo principal is that a refrain (here the "A" section) returns. Other rondo forms include: ABACBA (common in Mozart's music), ABACABA, and ABACADA.

14. <u>Rounded Binary</u>

A rounded binary form is a binary form piece that ends with an abbreviated return to the A section. Both the A and the B section are usually repeated. The form is diagramed as either: ABA'   or

$$\|: \text{A} :\| \qquad \|: \text{B A}' :\|$$

15. <u>Scherzo and trio</u>

The scherzo and trio often replaced the minuet and trio movement in the 19th century. It is in the same form as the minuet (see above, No. 9), but it is often faster and at times witty, or mannered. (*Scherzo* means "joke" in Italian.)

16. <u>Sonata Form</u>

The early history of sonata form is complex. For a detailed history, look at the article in the *NG*. In the 1740s binary forms of Neapolitan opera overtures began to use the principle of modulating to the dominant at the end of the A section. The B section would then begin in the dominant and modulate back to the tonic. By 1765 or so, the sonata form as we are taught it was the norm in the majority of fast movements from symphonies, sonatas, overtures, and other chamber works.

As early as 1755, various types of sonata-form movements were discussed by Joseph Riepel (1709-1782) in his treastise, *Fundamentals of the Ordering of Tones (Grundregeln zur Tonordnung insegemein)*. Although he does not call the forms "sonata", the types that he describes exhibit sonata principles.

In 1793, Heinrich Christoph Koch (1749-1816) describes sonata form in the third volume of his *Treatise of Instruction for Composition (Versuch einer Anleitung zur Composition)*. He does not name it, but the form is clearly developed.

The term, "sonata form" (*Sonatenform*) first appeared in a listing of Heinrich

---

Exposition

‖: <u>Theme I   transitional material   Theme II   Closing</u> :‖
‖ Tonic (I or i)   modulating to V (or III)   In V (or III) ------------------------ ‖

Development
Any themes from the exposition, or newly composed ones, may be used. The composer can modulate through any key as long as the tonic returns as the recapitulation begins.
<u>Many themes, new and/or old   </u>
Many keys, must return to --- (V of the tonic)

Recapitulation
<u>Theme I   transitional material   Theme II   Closing   Coda</u> ‖
Tonic --------   no modulation (still tonic) --- ‖

Birnbach's article in the table of contents of the *Berliner allgemeine musikalische Zeitung* of 1828 that Adolf Bernhard Marx (ca. 1795-1866) edited.

The traditional presentation of sonata form is presented below in a chart. The keys on the chart reflect a work in a major key as well as in a minor key, respectively.

17. <u>Sonata rondo</u>

This form combines sonata principles with the rondo refrain. Most often, the rondo form of ABACABA is used with the "B" section as the secondary key area and the "C" section as the development.

18. <u>Sonatina</u>

A work in a sonatina form usually follows the same pattern as one in sonata form but without a development section, and otherwise abbreviated.

19. <u>Song form</u>

This is a form of song popular in the 20th century that uses four groups of eight measures each following the format, AABA.

20. <u>Strophic form</u>

A strophic setting entails setting several stanzas of text (strophes) each to the same music. The composition, therefore, is a repetition of music with different stanzas of text. (The reader might recall hearing modern hymns or Christmas Carols which are often in strophic form, including several verses of text.) Visually, the form looks like this:

Music	A	A	A	A	A . . . .
Stanza of Text	A	B	C	D	E . . . .

21. <u>Strophic variations (strophic bass)</u>

Strophic variations were used in 17th-century vocal music. The aria's bass line is repeated for each stanza of text while different melodies are built above it. So, the piece is strophic, in that the bass line is the same for each stanza, but the melody is varied each time.

22. <u>Ternary Form</u>

Ternary Form implies a three-part form diagramed as: ABA
The ternary form, like the binary form, can have more complex internal organization.

23. <u>Theme and Variations</u>

A piece composed in a theme and variations format will present the listener first with the main theme(s) and then progress through a series of variations of that main melody.

24. <u>Through-composed form</u>

A through-composed piece does not utilize any repetition of significant musical material. In other words, it is composed from beginning to end without any large repetitions.

Chapter 5

ɔ୧

A Quick Survey of World Music

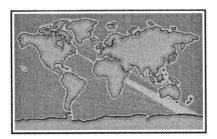

Attempting to learn the musical traits of every world culture is daunting to say the least. Ethnomusicologists often study in depth only a few music cultures in a lifetime of research. Yet, it is desirable to know at least the main features of as many music cultures as possible. This section is a brief and concise list of some of the more commonly known traits of several non-western,[1] world-music cultures. One book could not begin to discuss all of the music from all of the countries in our world.[2] In fact, even within one country, such as Mexico, Central Africa, China, etc, there are many music cultures not describable by merely one set of characteristics. Additionally, folk music in some countries can overlap the art music and even the popular music within that one community. And, within one geographic location there might be several music cultures, each with its own folk music, popular music *and* art music. So, although generalizations are necessary in order to gain any sort of overview, on the other hand, generalizations cannot begin to address the intricacies of music among so many people. That said, and for the sake of summary, this list should prove useful to students and teachers who are looking for a quick overview concerning the most popular world-music cultures that are studied in education today.

An important side note: We, in The United States, are a <u>concert culture</u>. We have concerts of rock music, classical music, church music, and other pop music. We value these events as the prices of tickets demonstrate. We grow up with band,

---

[1]*Non-Western* here refers to music that is not mostly produced through and by Western European art standards commonly taught in music history courses. Eastern Europe and Russia are often addressed in Western music history courses and will, for that reason, be omitted here.

[2]If the reader is interested in a particular country that is not listed here, the Internet can be a helpful source. The field of ethnomusicology continues to grow. And, with this growth, is a broader availability of current research. For instance, the music of Tibet is currently the subject of an organized project called, "Preserving Living Traditions." There is a website that gives the reader access to the most up-to-date information: http://www.thdl.org/collections/music/folkmusic.html

choir, and orchestra concerts and most states even have yearly contests for Junior High and Senior High School ensembles. We practice solo performances and are judged by professionals and audiences alike. Think about the premise of the recently popular TV show, "American Idol". It is based on a concert atmosphere, the performance of a singer within that media, and then the public judgment of the performance and performer. This is unique to *our* culture. Most non-Western music cultures do not have a concert-based music culture like ours, or if they do, they adapted our traditions, which ultimately are European. Keep that in mind as you read this chapter.

One more thing: Our Western classification of families of instruments (woodwinds, brass, percussion, strings) does not work well for the rest of the world's music. The world's classification system breaks down the groups of instruments into these four groups:

1. **Aerophones** are instruments that produce sound by using air as the primary source (that would include flutes, trumpets, a pipe organ, etc.).

2. **Chordophones** are instruments that produce sound from a vibrating string stretched between two points.

3. **Idiophones** are instruments that produce sound from the substance of the instrument itself. (Think xylophones, bells, cymbals, rattles.) **Metallophones** are instruments in this category that produce sound from vibrating metal bars that are struck with mallets.

4. **Membranophones** are instruments that are drum-like and produce their sounds from a tightly stretched membrane.

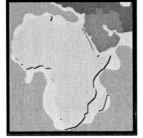

I. Africa[3]

Introductory Remarks:

There are more than 1000 tribes spread throughout Africa. There are hundreds of music cultures and many languages on the continent. Africa consists of about 55 countries, home to over 800 million people. Africa alone accounts for about one seventh of the world's population. Researchers, such as Ruth Stone, have stressed that African song, language, oral literature, instrumental music, theatre arts and dance are all a 'conceptual package' that most Africans conceive of as unitary.[4] Producing a list of musical characteristics that can generalize African music-culture can only be skeletal and extraordinarily broad. Many of the traits listed below refer to West African music in particular which has come to represent to us, the mainstream of African musical style.

African countries include: Algeria, Angola, Benin, Botswana, Burkina Faso, Burundi, Cameroon, Cape Verde, Central African Republic, Chad, Comoros, Congo (Brazzaville), Congo (DRC, Zaire), Cote d'Ivoire, Djibouti, Egypt, Equatorial Guinea, Eritrea, Ethiopia, Gabon, Gambia, Ghana, Guinea, Guinea-Bissaau, Kenya, Lesotho, Liberia, Libya, Madagascar, Malawi, Mali, Mauritania, Mauritius, Morocco, Mozambique, Namibia, Niger, Nigeria, Reunion, Rwanda, Sao Tome & Principe,

---

> (🌐) **Key Word Associations for Africa:** **polyrhythm, polyphony, call and response (antiphony), improvisation, music that is open to participation, oral tradition, percussive techniques, West-African drumming,** (instruments: **mbria, kora [cora]**)

Senegal, Seychelles, Sierra Leone, Somalia, South Africa, Sudan, Swaziland, Tanzania, Togo, Tunisia, Uganda, Western Sahara, Zambia, and Zimbabwe. Although each country within Africa deserves attention, for the sake of conciseness, only the general characteristics of the continent, as a whole, will be listed.

General Musical Characteristics:

1. There is often a call and response (antiphony) vocal presentation of songs.
2. The music can be highly complex rhythmically. Polyrhythms are common.
3. There are often syncopated beats and shifting accents within the rhythmic complexity. Percussive techniques are important whether they are created by

---

[3]The article in *The New Grove Dictionary of Music and Musicians,* "Africa" by Gerhard Kubik is well-organized, informative, and should be one of the reader's first choices for further research.

[4]Gerhard Kubrik, "Africa," *Grove Music Online* ed. L. Macy (Accessed 10, January 2006), <http://www.grovemusic.com>

drums, stomping, or hand clapping. African time in music is not the same as the concept of time in Western music.

4. The polyphony can be astonishing.[5]
5. There is a focus on singing and dancing together.
6. African music often happens in social situations where people's primary goals are not artistic.[6]
7. Music is not usually part of a concert event, but rather used in rituals, ceremonies, work, and play.
8. Repetition and improvisation play important roles.
9. There is an open quality to African music, inviting participation.
10. Musical training comes not from schools so much as it does from social participation in the culture.
11. Music is usually not held up as art, but rather is thought to be a necessary part of life, fused with other life processes or activities.
12. In some music cultures in Africa, music is an integral part of spiritual beliefs and religious ceremonies.
13. Several music cultures in Africa prefer to use a forceful chest voice, with no vibrato, when singing. The throat is tensed, symbolizing strength.
14. Harmony is an important part in the singing of a song.
15. West-African drumming has become popular worldwide.[7]

Instruments Used:[8]

1. **Bells** play an integral part in drum ensembles. The bells are the time-keepers of the beat. The bells can come in all sorts of shapes and sizes, including xylophone types such as the **bala**.
2. **Drums**: Information concerning drums and their usages in Africa could fill a book. Drum ensembles are popular. The ensemble usually plays an interweaving of patterns forming a complex, polyphonic fabric. The drums can be made of a variety of things and come in all sorts of sizes, shapes, and pitches.
3. The **Kora** (**Cora**) is a popular 21 stringed harp-lute played by Mandingo peoples throughout West Africa.
4. **Mbira**: The mbira is a popular instrument among some tribes, especially among the Shona people in Zimbabwe.
5. **Rattles** are as common as are bells. They too, come in all sorts of shapes and sizes. A **Shekere** is one type.

---

[5]There is a good Internet article concerning the Ewe culture and rhythmic principles in its music by C. K. Ladzekpo, a native Ewe man. http://www.cnmat.berkeley.edu/~ladzekpo/Intro.html.
[6]J. T. Titon, *Worlds of Music*, Chapter 3 by David Locke, Thompson Schirmer, 2005, p. 75.
[7]See: http://www.sbgmusic.com/html/teacher/reference/cultures/westafr.html.
[8]These sites offer short MP3 files and other images of some African instruments. http://www.ncf.ca/~el965/instruments/#berimbau and http://www.cnmat.berkeley.edu/%7Eladzekpo/ and http://digi-coll.library.wisc.edu/AfricaFocus/

6. North African instruments can include instruments common to the Arabic nations such as **water drums**, reed instruments (double clarinet, shawm), **rabab**, lutes, tambourines, **santur**, **tambur**, and fiddles.

Tonal System:

Sometimes the tonal systems of certain music cultures in Africa seem vague because of the lack of instrumental accompaniment, which would have produced precise pitch points. Often songs are produced only vocally and seem to aim for pitch areas rather than pitch points.[9] Recently, European instruments have brought Western tonality to the continent. This tonality has sometimes mixed with the more indigenous sort of tonality that had previously resulted out of certain African speech patterns.[10]

II. North America

A. Native American Music

Introductory Remarks:

There are more than 500 Native American tribes in the United States with about 300 reservations (not every tribe is recognized by the government), 12 of which are larger than the state of Rhode Island. Needless to say, the variety of music cultures within these communities is great. Some of the first Native American music to be heard in Western Europe was recorded on wax cylinder in the early 1900s. The music was played in Berlin to an amazed audience. The non-Western characteristics of that music still exist in some of the traditional music of Native America.

Typically, scholars have divided the many Native American groups in North American into six regions: Eastern Woodlands, Plains, Southwest, Great Basin, Northwest Coast, and Arctic.

> **Key Word Associations for Native American Music:** **vocables, pulsating drum beats, oral tradition, tetratonic, pentatonic** (instruments: **drums and rattles, Peyote rattle, water drum, flutes**)

General Musical Characteristics:

1. Music in Native American culture accompanies most aspects of life.
2. The music is usually monophonic, focused on vocal presentation, accompanied often by drums and rattles.
3. Singers often use meaningless syllables of words, rather than actual language (J. T. Titon calls these "vocables").
4. There is prominent repetition of text. Many songs are strophic.
5. The rhythm is often pulsated with driving drum beats.

---

[9] Titon, p. 85.
[10] *Ibid.*

6. Sometimes the singers use a piercing falsetto voice, often leaping more than an octave.
7. Phrases are typically short, and well-articulated.
8. The music is mostly preserved in society through oral tradition and memory instead of through a written musical notation.
9. Instrumental ensemble music, as in Western classical traditions, was unknown until the Europeans' instruments were incorporated about 40 or 50 years ago.

Instruments Used:

Sometimes the instruments in this music culture have spiritual meaning or significance.
1. Drums (simple **skin drums**, **water drums**, frame drums, and square drums)
2. Rattles (container rattles: deer hoof rattles, cow-horn rattles, **Peyote rattle**)
3. Flutes (wood, clay, bone, bamboo)
4. clapper sticks

Tonal System:

1. Many songs are based on tetratonic (four-note) or pentatonic (five note) scales.
2. The music of Native America has often been described as modal.

Specific Details:

Songs from the <u>Eastern Woodlands</u> area use antiphony (call and response). Among Native American music, antiphony is exclusive to this area. Some instrumental music is performed, primarily with flutes and whistles.

The <u>Plains</u> vocal style is nasal and extraordinarily agitated. Singers emphasize the high range, often using falsetto. One of the striking characteristics of this style is the simultaneous playing of a large drum by all singers in the group.

The Pueblo musicians of the <u>Southwest</u> use a relaxed vocal style, singing relatively slow songs. The Navajo and Apache musicians of the Southwest area, use a tense, nasal voice, similar to the Plains style. The Apache fiddle is unique to this culture and is used as a solo instrument.

The singing style of the <u>Great Basin</u> is relaxed with short melodies having a range smaller than an octave. This music contains a rhythmic complexity that uses micro-rhythms produced during the use of special breathing techniques.

Within the <u>Northwest Coast</u> repertoire there are examples of part-singing. This is the only Native American music culture in which we find music more complex than monophony. The melodies are long with chromatic intervals, a rarity in Native America.

The <u>Arctic</u> area includes diverse cultures formerly identified under one designation, Eskimos. The singing style is slightly tense, and Arctic singers are known for their use of extended vocal techniques.[11] Shallow hand drums that resemble tambourines are unique to this area.

B. Black American Music

Introductory Remarks:

Characteristics from this music culture can be traced to those of the Caribbean and Africa. Some have suggested that music in Africa, used to ease the pain of work, moved into America as work songs and the Blues. Music for worship in various African cultures was diffused into gospel traditions in The United States. The important tradition of drumming, especially as a form of communication, came to America resulting in strong rhythmic qualities in Black American music.

The Minstrel entertainments in America, beginning in the 1830s, were shows in which white men dressed up as black slaves and imitated African and African American folk song and dance. This strange, and shameful, phenomenon exposed this country to a new world of music and traditions belonging to the new Black Americans. (By the way, these shows remained popular until the 1950s!)

General Musical Characteristics:

1. Music is used by people engaged in work, worship, and play.
2. This music is unique in style and is neither African nor European.
3. There is an importance placed on improvisation and also on emotional involvement.
4. Antiphony is common (call-and-response).
5. Work songs were widely used by black slaves.
6. Rhythm is extremely important and often syncopated.

Tonal System:

The tonality of Black-American music is mostly diatonic. Notes within diatonicism are manipulated for stylistic effects, such as in the blues scale. Here, the seventh and third scale degrees are slightly altered.

Specific Details:

Look at Chapter 6, "A Quick Look at Jazz History".

---

[11]http://college.hmco.com/history/readerscomp/naind/html/na 024300_ music.htm, accessed January 6, 2006.

III. Asia

Introductory Remarks:

Asia is earth's largest continent including about 44 countries and assorted islands. Asia has three divisions:

1. **The Middle East** (or West Asia) including Armenia, Azerbaijan, Afghanistan, Bahrain, Egypt (considered to be in both in Africa and in the Middle East), Georgia, Iran, Iraq, Israel, Jordon, Kuwait, Kyrgyzstan, Lebanon, Oman, Pakistan, Qatar, Saudi Arabia, Syria. Tajikistan, Turkey, Turkmenistan, United Arab Emirates, Uzbekistan, and Yemen.
2. **Southeast Asia** (or South Asia) including Bangladesh, Bhutan, Brunei, Burma, Cambodia, East Timor, India, Indonesia, Laos, Malaysia, Maldives, Myanmar, Nepal, Philippines, Singapore, Sri Lanka, Thailand, and Vietnam.
3. **North Asia** including China, Eastern Europe, Japan (sometimes referred to alone as **East Asia**), Kazakhstan, Mongolia, North Korea, Russian Federation, South Korea, and Taiwan.

In ethnomusicology, several primary countries of Asia are studied more than others in world-music survey courses. Furthermore, typically, Russia and Eastern Europe are studied apart from Asia. The following list is a presentation of some of the more widely-known information.

A. China

Introductory Remarks

China is home to over one billion people, the most populated country on the planet. Naturally, a list of characteristics will be general rather than specific. There are three types of music in China: classical (art) music, folk music, and pop music.[12] One helpful survey on the topic is William Alves' *Music of the Peoples of the World*, (2006 by Cengage Publishing), Chapter Six, *China*.

> 🌐 **Key Word Associations for China:** heterophony, delicate timbre changes, intricate ornamentation, Beijing opera, (instruments: **xiao (bamboo flutes), sheng, erhu, Qin (Guqin)**)

General Musical Characteristics:

1. Much of the music is monophonic, either for voice or for an instrument.
2. The melody, when accompanied, is often performed in heterophony.[13]

---

[12]To learn about the latter see the website: http://www.chinasite.com/Entertainment/Music.html
[13]See Chapter 1 of this book for a review of textures.

3. The musical forms often are based on the notion of variation. Sets of elaborate variations of a particular melody are common.

4. Because the music is so focused on melody, intricate ornamentation is added. The types of ornamentation can be specific to a particular instrument.

5. Differences in timbre (colors of sounds) are just as important to a piece of music as is the actual melody. Minute differences in timbre occur on single pitches. This is true also concerning some Asian spoken languages and Chinese music is related to the Chinese language. In language, which uses tonality, a different pitch on the same word can indicate a different meaning. Color in music is used in a similar way.

6. Balance is important in all things.

7. Sometimes Chinese art music can have poetic associations or titles.

8. Silence is used (often at the ends of phrases) as a means of poetic/artistic reflection and expression.

9. Although the use of pentatonic scales is often associated with Chinese music, it is only one aspect of their tonality.

10. Most Chinese music (when metrical) favors duple rhythm with syncopations being common.

11. Although there are regional differences, the style of singing is often characterized as more high-pitched and nasal than the style of Western music.

12. Chinese opera (drama) is popular and found in many varieties. Beijing opera is the most widely performed. It combines singing of songs, speech, dance, instrumental music, elaborate costumes, and martial arts.

Instruments Used:

There are *thousands* of instruments in China. Stringed and wind instruments are the most common types. Some instruments have developed their own notation and instruments are often associated with particular social classes or with certain functions of a piece of music. Here are just a few of the most popular instruments.

1. **Di (dixi)**: a side held (traverse) bamboo flute, and the most popular type of traverse flute in China. Rice paper covers one hole to give the instrument a certain buzz when played.

2. **Erhu**: a two-stringed bowed instrument with no fingerboard. The hair of the bow is threaded between the two strings of the instrument.

3. **Gao-Hu**: a fiddle.

4. **Guan**: a cylinder fitted with a reed mouthpiece creating a nasal sound. It comes in a variety of sizes and a variety of types according to geographic location.

5. **Jing-Hu**: a Peking opera fiddle that is high pitched and vigorous in timbre.

6. **Paixiao**: a set of end blown bamboo panpipes that uses rice paper to cover one hole, giving it a buzz when played.

7. Many types of Percussion including: gongs (**luo**), bells, cymbals (**bo**), wood blocks, drums, stones (**Pien Ching**).[14]
8. **Pipa**: a lute with frets and four strings held upright when played. It is usually plucked. Often, pieces for this instrument are programmatic in nature.
9. **Qin** (**Guqin**): a zither with seven silk strings stretched over a hollow wooden box nearly four feet long. Confucius favored the instrument and it can be dated back at least 3000 years. It is considered to be the instrument of scholars.
10. **Ruan**: a rounded four-stringed lute resembling the shape of a large banjo.
11. **Sheng**: a pan pipe; a bundle of 17 to 36 different pipes. It comes in several ranges from low to high.
12. **Suona** (**laba**): a loud double-reed instrument played vertically that is associated with folk music and outdoor ceremonies.
13. **Yangqin**: a hammered dulcimer of sorts, in the shape of a trapezoid. The hammers are usually thin bamboo sticks.
14. **Xiao**: a vertically held bamboo flute. It can come in a variety of sizes like a recorder.
15. **Xun**: a flute made of clay.
16. **Zheng** (**Guzheng**): a zither (looks similar to a dulcimer) with 21 strings. The strings are usually plucked with plectra (picks).

Tonal System:

1. Chinese music uses several types of pentatonic scales (five-note scales) and several types of seven-note scales.
2. The majority of the music is not based on triads and will not be heard as chordal. (Our Western music is chordal and based on triads.)

B. Japan

Introductory Remarks:

There are several thousand islands that make up the Japanese archipelago (a sea with many islands, or the islands within that sea). The four largest islands in Japan are Honshu, Hokkaido, Kyushu and Shikoku. In this country that sprawls from the north to the south over 1200 miles, there is a rich array of modern and traditional music cultures. Traditional Japanese culture embraces two types of music: folk music and art music. Today, the country is a mix of Eastern and Western cultures with technologically advanced cities that combine old and new styles. Apart from Western influences, traditional music of Japan is fostered among the public in an attempt to continue the appreciation for Japanese history and culture. (There are even televised contests of folk-song singing.) Japanese music of the past is respected and fostered for its artistic importance, much like the European music is among Westerners.

---

[14]A concise and more detailed look at a Chinese orchestra is at the site: http://www.chinesemusic. co.uk/ english/InstrumentsPage.htm

---

🌐 <u>**Key Word Associations for Japan**</u>: **pentatonic based scales, monophonic and heterophonic textures, slow pitch movement, free rhythm, Taiko drumming, kouta, gagaku, enka, *No* theater, *Kabuki* theater, Karaoke,** (instruments: **koto, Shakuhachi, shamisen**)

General Musical Characteristics:

1. There is a diversity of scale tuning systems, often with the pentatonic scale as the foundation.
2. There is not a particular set of pitches that is used by all musicians. Rather, the exact pitch intervals differ in traditional music according to the genre, the style of the music, and even the particular performer.
3. Additionally, scholars do not agree on the particular details about how certain scale systems actually work. (So expect this to be an obstacle if you choose to study Japanese music.)
4. There is a special use of monophonic and heterophonic textures in traditional Japanese music. Homophony is present in some of Japan's music that has been influenced by the West.
5. Some vocal music utilizes elaborate ornamentation.
6. Pitch movement in the music can seem slow compared to that of Western music.
7. Monophonic melodies tend to emphasize intervals of the fourth.
8. Un-pitched sounds, such as breath noises or string noises, are common in instrumental melodies. (Exhaling is an important aspect in Zen Buddhism, and thus often, in music).
9. Metrical organization of the beats into a steady pulse is often missing in Japanese music. Even if a steady beat is present, there is flexibility within the tempo.
10. The tempo is accelerated when the musicians want to create excitement.
11. Japanese folk music uses a type of singing that tends to be strong and declamatory with slides, pitched shouts, and melismatic passages.
12. *Taiko* drumming and the ensembles who perform, have become symbols of Japan's musical tradition. There are about 1,500 taiko groups in Japan and another 150 in the United Sates and Canada.

Important Genres

1. *Koutas* are Japanese songs that date from the 19th century. These popular songs, often heterophonic, were intended for women singers and were sung to the accompaniment of the *shamisen*.
2. Traditional work songs called *minyo* are still popular in Japan today.
3. *Enka* songs developed in the 19th century as a new type of political statement. Today, *enkas* are the songs of choice for the popular pastime of Karaoke.

4. Ancient Imperial court music is called *gagaku*. It is the oldest type of traditional Japanese music.

5. *Noh* [also *No*] *theater* is a very old form of traditional Japanese theater in which the actors wear masks while speaking and singing in a monotonous way, accompanied by a chorus and traditional instruments.

6. *Nogaku* is music played during *No* performances. It consists of a chorus, the *Hayashi flute*, the *Tsuzumi drum*, and other instruments.

7. *Kabuki theater* is a traditional Japanese form of theater, based on historical events and presented in ancient language. The performance is intended for the townspeople, not the aristocracy.

Instruments Used:

Japanese music uses three basic types of instruments: stringed, wind, and percussion.

1. **Biwa**: a short-necked lute; used since the 7th century in *gagaku*.

2. **Koto**: a 13-stringed instrument that is about six feet long; the strings are usually plucked with picks called *tsume* that are attached to the thumb, index and middle finger of the right hand; the left hand touches the strings to alter pitch and timbre.

3. **Nokan**: a flute used in *Noh* theatrical performances.

4. **Sankyoku**: this is an ensemble of a **koto**, **shamisen**, and **shakuhachi**.

5. **Shakuhachi**: a bamboo flute that is linked to Zen Buddhism; this instrument is a spiritual tool according to ancient beliefs.

6. **Shamisen**: a three-stringed long-necked zither (think lute-like); the strings can be plucked or struck; there is a special buzz called *sawari* which is purposefully added to the instrument when it is made; it is an instrument commonly used in the productions of *bunraku puppet theater.*

7. **Taiko**: drums; the big drum is called **Odaiko**; the hourglass shaped drums are called **tsuzumi**, with the smaller **kotsuzumi** and the larger **otsuzumi** both popular in *noh* (also *no*) and *kabuki* theatrical performances.

8. **Takebue** and **shinobue**: two side-blown flutes often heard during festivals.

Tonal System:

Only the Western-influenced Japanese music uses our Western tonality. All of the traditional music is based on complex systems of scales that are not based on a Western tuning system of equal intervals within the octave. Consequently, quarter-tones are prevalent.

C. India

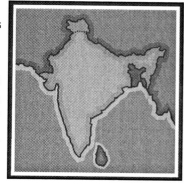

Introductory Remarks:

India is large and diverse. It is the second most populous country in the world, second only to China. There are regional differences between the classical music styles of northern and southern India. Classical music in South India is called *Carnatic* music (also called *karnataka sangeeta*) while the classical musical style of North India is called *Hindustani* music. Both styles uses the idea of the *raga* (think melodic mode) and *tala* (think metric cycle), but the specifics of the *ragas* and *talas* vary.

> 🌐 **Key Word Associations for India:** **raga, tala, melakarta system, carnatic, Hindustani, kriti,** (instruments: **sitar, tabla, veena, punji, santur**)

General Musical Characteristics:

1. Indian music has been transmitted primarily through memory and oral tradition.
2. Improvisation plays a key role in performance.
3. Drones are often used, providing a sustained tonal center.
4. There is an ancient belief that music can never be frozen in time. This means that music cannot exist in notation.
5. North Indian music uses the **sitar** and **tabla**.
6. One type of Northern music, the *Hindustani style*, is expansive in its improvisations, sometimes lasting an hour or more. The music begins with very little movement and gradually gains speed and virtuosity over great lengths (*hours*) of time.
7. South Indian music (*Carnatic* music) is more conservative than the Northern style in that it is built around an existing repertoire of Hindu devotional songs.
8. Indian culture embraces concerts of Indian music, but the concerts are not as formally organized as American types.
9. Most Indian music is built in layers: the background drone (called the *sruti* layer), the melodic layer, and the rhythmic layer.
10. The percussive (rhythmic) layer holds the ensemble together. *Tala* is the organization of time in music. The beats for the performers are grouped into regularly recurring metric cycles. These cycles are called *tala* and the drummer's art is extraordinarily complex, holding the ensemble together.

Important Genres

The *kriti* is the principle song form of South Indian classical music.

Instruments Used:

1. **Jalatarangam**: an instrument that is made of porcelain bowls filled with different amounts of water to create a specific tuning; the bowls are struck with two thin sticks.
2. **Kanjira**: a percussive instrument like a tambourine made of wood and lizard skin with attached jangles.
3. **Kudam**: a single-stringed folk instrument made of a clay pot and wooden board.
4. **Mridangam**: the primary drum (two-headed) in South Indian music.
5. **Nagasvaram**: a double reed pipe that is about three feet long.
6. **Punji**: a reed instrument (single or double) with two pipes, one of which is a drone; it is the instrument played by snake charmers.
7. **Santoor** (**Santur**): a hammered dulcimer in the shape of a trapezoid; the instrument is popular in Kashmir.
8. **Shahnai**: a double reed instrument similar to an oboe and used in North India.
9. **Shanku**: a conch shell trumpet used for important events in the court and in the temple.
10. **Sitar**: a 22-stringed instrument that is plucked; it is one of the most popular classical instruments of North India.
11. **Sruti-box**: a drone instrument that works like a small reed organ by pumping bellows.
12. **Tabla**: the principal drum instrument in North India; it has two small drums, one metal and the other wood.
13. **Tambura**: a four-stringed lute that is plucked; it often plays the drone.
14. **Tavil**: a double-headed drum.
15. **Veena**: a seven stringed plucked instrument; the instrument is extremely large with 24 frets and a large resonating bowl.

Tonal System:

The tonal system of India is one of the world's most complex. The music is based on the *raga* melodic system, which has no equivalent in the West. There are many *ragas* with rules for each about how a musician may move from one note to another and even how he is to create ornamentation. *Ragas* are taught orally by a master to his student over an extended number of years. Tradition associates certain *ragas* with particular human emotions, *(rasas)*, that are generated by works of art. The ten human emotions *(rasas)* are: love, sadness, heroism, anger, fear, disgust, wonder, laughter, religious devotion, and peacefulness. Additionally, *ragas* are associated with seasons, times of the day, colors, animals, deities, and powers such as the causing of rain or warmth. To complicate matters further, in *Carnatic* music (southern Indian music) all *ragas* are related to a *melakarta* system. This system contains 72 basic scales of seven tones each. The performer then transforms a *melakarta* scale into a *raga* according to the rules and characteristics of that particular *raga* which then has its own characteristics of intonation, melodic motives, and ornamentations. Incredibly, the Indian tonal and musical system is actually far more complicated than I have described here.

D. Indonesia

Introductory Remarks:

Indonesia is an archipelago in Southeast Asia consisting of over 17,000 islands. Of those thousands of islands, only about 6,000 are inhabited, the largest of which are Java, Sumatra, Bali, Kalimantan, Sulawesi, the Nusa Tenggara islands, the Moluccas Islands, West Papua, and the western part of New Guinea. With islands of such diversity, the music cultures of Indonesia are numerous. There are large cities with Western style discos, aristocratic Javaense gamelans, rural farms, and even technology-void tribes. Many countries including, Portugal, Japan, Britain, The Netherlands, and India have claimed reign on and off throughout Indonesia's history. The country has experienced a great deal of political unrest and natural disasters over the years. There is no one culture of Indonesia that is representative of the whole. Therefore, the following characteristics are a conglomeration of current ethnomusicological research.

> **Key Word Associations for Indonesia: Javanese and Balinese gamelans, shadow puppetry (wayang kulit), colotomic structure, slendro, pelog, barong dance of Bali, tembang sunda, kecapi suling**

General Musical Characteristics:

1. Javanese gamelans have become popular worldwide. The word gamelan refers to a set of instruments, usually gongs, bells, and drums, which are unified by their tuning systems. The music is either loud or soft and is layered with a main melody and rhythmic patterns containing punctuations. The size and instrumental composition of gamelans vary. They can contain winds, strings, and xylophone-like instruments.[15]

2. There are also gamelans in Bali, which differ slightly from those in Java. One difference is that the Balinese gamelans use cymbals and the Javanese gamelans do not.

3. The shadow puppet theater (*wayang kulit*) is popular, and is often associated with the music of a gamelan. These performances can last for hours with one master puppeteer directing all aspects of the performance.

---

[15]See Titon, pages 233-249 for details.

4. There is a tradition of unaccompanied singing called *tembang sunda*. The wordsactually mean *sung poetry*.

5. *Kecapi suling* is a type of instrumental music. It is highly improvisational and related to *tembang sunda*.

6. Certain instruments, particularly gongs, have religious functions for Muslim holy days.

7. In Bali, artistic beauty is cultivated with elaborate costumes and Balinese shadow puppetry.

8. *Angklung* are instruments made of bamboo. It also refers to a sort of music that uses bamboo instruments.

9. Colotomic structures are used in gamelan music. A colotomic structure is created when instruments are used to regularly punctuate certain moments in the metrical cycle. For instance, a gong might punctuate every 8, 16, 32, 64 beats while a different instrument punctuates every 2, 4, 8, 16 beats. There are layers of punctuation that create a complex rhythmic relationship in the ensemble.

10. In Bali, there is a type of music called *kecak* (*cak*) that is purely vocal and performed by men singing, shouting, speaking, and chanting.[16]

11. The *barong* dance of Bali is a dance-drama of a mythical dragon-like creature that is the holy protector of a village.

Instruments Used:

1. **In the Javanese gamelan:**

   a. **Bonang:** a set of gong chimes with ten to fourteen kettles.

   b. **Celempung:** a plucked zither on four legs raised up from the back; there are thirteen pairs of strings.

   c. **Gambang:** a wooden xylophone with a range of two octaves or more.

   d. **Gender:** a metallophone with bronze keys.

   e. **Gong:** the largest gong that hangs; it has the lowest pitch.

   f. **Kempul:** smaller hanging gongs.

   g. **Kendhang:** a two-headed, barrel shaped drum.

   h. **Kenong:** a set of large kettledrums.

   i. **Kethuk:** a small kettledrum.

   j. **Rebab:** a two-stringed bowed lute-like instrument with a body of wood with a stretched membrane.

   k. **Saron:** a metallophone that is often given the melody; it usually has only six or seven keys (bars).

   l. **Siyem:** the second largest hanging gong, next to the gong.

   m. **Slenthem:** a metallophone that is often given the melody.

   n. **Suling:** bamboo flutes.

---

[16] See Alves, pages 244-248 for details.

2. **In the Balinese gamelan:**
   a. **Cymbals**
   b. **Jegogan:** it is the lowest pitched of the instruments with long resonating bamboo tubes; it often punctuates with the gongs.
   c. **Jublag:** it is an instrument with long resonating bamboo tubes pitched one octave higher than the jegogan; it is used more frequently than the jegogan and less frequently than the ugal; sometimes the jublag takes the melody from the ugal with which it shares pitches.
   d. **Kantil:** a higher pitched instrument with very short resonating bamboo tubes; it is higher than the ugal.
   e. **Pemade:** the pemade is pitched an octave above the ugal; it is made of short resonating bamboo tubes; it shares its upper octave with the kantil and its lower octave with the ugal.
   f. **Reyong:** this is a series of small horizontal gongs arranged in a straight line; it is played by two or four players and spans more than several octaves.
   g. **Ugal:** an instrument with large resonating bamboo tubes; it often carries the melody in the ensemble, spanning two octaves.

Tonal System:

There are two primary tuning systems for gamelan instruments, neither of which are Western. One system is called *slendro* and is based on a five-tone system of nearly equidistant intervals. The other system is called *pelog* and is based on seven tones of large and small intervals. Neither scale can be played on a Western keyboard and there can even be variation in the pitches between gamelan ensembles.

E. Iran

Introductory Remarks:

Arabic music shares certain common characteristics. The music of Iran will serve as an example here.

> 🌐 **Key Word Associations for Arabic Music: maqam (maqamat, plural), iqu' (iqu'at, plural), wazn (plural, awzān), qira'ah (or tilawah), quartertones (microtones)** (instruments: **'ud, nay, qanun, riq, santur, tar**)

General Musical Characteristics:

1. Classical Iranian music contains ornate melodies that are improvised and decorated with motives. There is an absence of polyphony, polyrhythm, and traditional motivic development.
2. There is a predominance of vocal music, particularly with elaborate melismas. (Remember that a melisma is a vocal melody sung with many notes on one syllable of text.)
3. Heterophony plays an important role. Melodies are presented with simultaneous presentations of decorated versions of the same melody.

4. There is an emphasis on melody and rhythm rather than on harmony.
5. Improvisation is central to the music.
6. Beat patterns are used as a basis for rhythmic patterns. Ostinatos are common.
7. Microtones (quarter tones) are part of the tonal system.
8. Islamic chanting in religious ceremonies is not considered to be music by the participants, but is viewed by an outsider as singing of chants. Verses chanted from the *Qur'an* (*Koran*, the *Holy Book of Isalm*) are known as **qira'ah or tilawah**.
9. An *adhan* is a call to prayer presented by the *mu'adhdhin* over loud speakers.
10. Arabic classical music strives to create a feeling of *tarab*, which is a transcendent emotional state.
11. Bowed instruments often accompany a solo singer; the singer often accompanies himself.
12. Responsorial and antiphonal practices are important.
13. The **maqam** is the tonal basis of Arabic music, consisting of a set of modes/scales that utilize quartertones.
14. Improvisations on a solo instrument are called *taqsim* when they are used to help establish an introduction to a scale of the *maqam*. The improvisations of a vocalist are called *layali*.
15. Rhythm in Arabic music is influenced by complex meters of classical Arabic poetry. **Metric modes** are used in various metric compositions and are widely known by the name **iqa'at** (singular **iqa'**).
16. A **wazn** (plural, **awzān**) is a rhythmic pattern or cycle. There are about 100 different cycles used in Arabic music.

Instruments Used:

1. **Arghul:** a single reed instrument with two cylindrical pipes tied together like an ancient aulos; it is popular in Egypt.
2. **Daff (Duf):** a shallow frame drum.
3. **Darabukkah:** a goblet-shaped drum; it can come in a variety of sizes and materials; also called **tabla**; It is known as the **zarb** or **tombak** in Iran.
4. **Harp**
5. **Kaman:** a European violin.
6. **Kamanche:** a small short-necked fiddle with a pear-shaped body.
7. **Lyre**
8. **Nay:** an end-blown flute that is played from the side of the mouth; it is the only aerophone that is regularly found in Iranian classical ensembles.[17]
9. **Qanun:** a plucked zither which is similar to a psaltery; it has 26 courses of triple strings.
10. **Rabab:** a small bowed fiddle with one to four strings; it is a common folk instrument.
11. **Riq:** a tambourine with five sets of heavy brass cymbals.

---

[17]See Alves, page 85.

12. **Santur:** a trapezoidal hammered zither (dulcimer); the instrument is common in China, India, Europe, and other places as well.
13. **Tanbur:** a long-necked lute.
14. **Tar:** the classical plucked lute from Iran; it has an hourglass shaped body.
15. **'Ud:** a short-necked lute with five pairs of strings.
16. **Zurna:** a loud double-reed similar to a shawm which was an ancestor of the oboe.

Tonal System:

Ancient improvisation and composition were based on modes called *echoi*. Today, the modal system is known as the *maqam*. There are 24 notes per octave, thus creating a system of quartertones. There is not agreement as to whether these quartertones must be equidistant from each other. Each quartertone scale has its own name. Notation throughout the Arabic countries is not standardized. Smaller segments (usually tetrachords, trichords, or pentachords) are used to build the scales.

IV. Latin America

Introductory Remarks:

There are many countries in Latin America and the Caribbean. Central American countries include, Belize, Costa Rica, El Salvador, Guatemala, Honduras, Nicaragua, and Panama. South American countries include, Argentina, Bolivia, Brazil, Chile, Colombia, Ecuador, French Guiana, Guyana, Paraguay, Peru, Suriname, Uruguay, and Venezuela. Mexico is part of North America and is perhaps the most influential Latin American country. Caribbean countries include, Antiqua & Barbuda, Aruba, Bahamas, Barbados, Cayman Islands, Cuba, Dominica, Dominican Republic, Grenada, Guadeloupe, Haiti, Jamaica, Matinique, Puerto Rico, St. Kitts & Mevis, St. Lucia, St. Vincent and the Grenadines, Trinidat & Tobago, Turks & Caicos Islands, and Virgin Islands. Obviously, there are hundreds of music cultures thriving in Latin America. The music of Brazil and Mexico can serve as a nice introduction to the area.

A. Brazil

Introductory Remarks:

Brazil won its independence from Portugal in 1822. It is the largest country in Latin America and the only one to have not been colonized by the Spanish. Brazil has a classical musical tradition that dates back to the Renaissance. Portuguese musicians brought with them to Brazil their own traditions. But the indigenous music of Brazil is more complex. The Native people of Brazil play instruments such as flutes, drums, rattles, and horns, imitating sounds that one might encounter in the Amazon Rainforest. In addition to the Native Brazilians and the Portuguese, there are also musical traditions of African music from the African slaves that were brought to the country.

🌐 **Key Word Associations for Brazil: choro, samba, bossa nova,** (instruments: **batucada, carimbo, cavaquinho**)

General Musical Characteristics:

1. Music with dance is common and Brazilian music is often characterized by interesting and invigorating dance rhythms.[18]
2. A **carimbo** is an African drum. It is also the name of a Brazilian dance during which a woman drops a handkerchief to the floor, which must then be picked up by a man using only his mouth. This dance music continued in popularity and eventually was incorporated into pop culture.
3. The carnival celebrations of Parintins (a city) focus on folk music of Brazil.
4. *Choro* is a popular musical style of Brazil that had its roots in 19th-century Rio de Janeiro (a city). *Choro* originally was played by a trio (guitar, flute, and **cavaquinho** [a small four-stringed- instrument]). Today, the style has evolved into additional new styles and the instrumental make-up is expanded. *Choro* is typically instrumental and based largely on improvisation.
5. The *Samba* came out of the *choro* in the early 20th century and is probably Brazil's most popular dance music. It was popular originally among poor blacks who descended from slaves. Today, there are several types of *samba*. Elements of a *samba* include its 2/4 meter with the strongest accent on the second beat and a stanza and refrain structure with a concentration of interlocking and syncopated rhythms.
6. The *bossa nova* (the new beat) mixes a *samba* beat with a popular jazz style. The *bossa nova* style developed in the beach communities of Ipanema and in the Copacabana nightclubs. The rhythm is a 2 + 3 + 3 grouping, often notated as a quarter note followed by two dotted quarter notes.
7. Afro-Brazilian music is popular today throughout the country.

Instruments Used:

1. The **batucada** is the ensemble of percussion instruments that often play samba.
2. **Berimbau**: a one-stringed instrument that is shaped like a bow; a gourd is attached to the bow to create a special resonance; it came from Africa and was used originally by slaves to accompany the famous dance called *Capoeira*.
3. **Carimbos** are large drums of African origin.
4. A **Cavaquinho** is a type of **ukulele**.
5. **Guitars** of various types.

---

[18]See William Alves, *Music of the Peoples of the World*, page 299 for more details concerning types of samba ostinatos.

6. **Percussion** of all sorts including drums, tambourines, and bells.

Tonal System:

The tonal system of Brazil is based primarily upon European tonality as it was imported by the Portuguese. Additionally, African influences introduced modal systems.

B. Mexico

Introductory Remarks:

Mexico is the most populous Spanish-speaking country in the world containing about 106 million people. Mexico is divided into 31 states and a federal district where the government in Mexico City is located. The country is about one-fourth the size of the US and contains rain forests, deserts, beaches, farms, and large cities.

> **Key Word Associations for Mexico: mariachi, ranchera, norteño, Mexican son, tejano, arribeño, conjunto jarocho, topada,** (instruments: **bandolon, marimba, vihuela, guitarrón, accordian**)

General Musical Characteristics:

1. It is a common belief that music is a natural expression of the "Mexican soul".
2. Mexico's music has been influenced by European, Cuban, and African cultures.
3. Parallel thirds are used to thicken the harmonic textures in vocal music. Harmony is very important.
4. Distinctive dance rhythms pervade much music of Latin America in general. Two popular dances include the habañera and the sesqualtera.[19]
5. The guitar, and instruments similar to it, adds "vigorous harmonic strumming" that emphasize dance rhythms.[20] The strumming of chords creates a mostly homophonic texture.
6. *Mariachi* is the most famous sort of Mexican folk music. It typically is performed by an ensemble band of five or more playing trumpets, violins, guitars (often the *vihuela* and the *guitarrón*). The group can also utilize singers.
7. *Conjunto jarocho* is a genre of music similar to Mariachi. It has its origin in Veracruz and Tabasco near the Bay of Campeche.
8. Shouts and cries are added to folk music to create a vigorous character.

---

[19] See Alves, p. 284, for a nice chart of Latin American dances and their origins.
[20] Alves, p. 283.

9. *Ranchera* (ranch songs) were popular during the Mexican Revolution (1910). The songs dealt with rural live and unrequited love and often contained the text, "ay, ay, ay, ay, ay". Mariachi bands often play these songs.

10. *Norteño* is a genre popular in Northern Mexico that utilizes an accordion and a large 12-stringed guitar called the *bajo sexto*. The bands can be very large including brass and string sections. The music is similar to *Tejano* music and it originated in the 1830s near the southern border of Texas.

11. *Mexican son* originated in the eighteenth century as a large and inclusive genre of folk music that encouraged audience participation for a foot stamping rhythmic part. Mariachi music is one type of Mexican son. The term *son* includes a number of regional music and dance traditions, each with its own particular traditions.

12. *Arribeño* is a competitive genre of music and poetry performed (and judged) at a competition called *topada*. Musician-poets are judged on their poetry, which is intended to be personal, and their musical presentation of the verses.

Instruments Used:

1. **Accordian**
2. **Bajo sexto**: a 12-stringed bass guitar.
3. **Bandolon**: an oval-shaped guitar with eighteen strings.
4. **Guitarra de son**: (Sometimes called *requinto jarocho*) is made from a single piece of wood and comes in a variety of sizes. It can be plucked or strummed.
5. **Guitarrón**: a six-stringed bass guitar.
6. **Harp** (arpa)
7. **Jarana**: a guitar-like instrument with five courses, three of which may be doubled, resulting in eight strings. It comes in a variety of sizes and names.
8. **Marimba**: a xylophone type instrument with wooden keys (bars) that are struck with mallets. Metal tubes are located under the wooden bars, giving the instrument a rich resonation.
9. **Percussion**: including a wide variety of drums, tambourines, and shakers (including *maracas*).
10. **Trumpets**
11. **Vihuela**: a five-stringed strummed guitar-like instrument.
12. **Violin**

Tonal System:

The tonal system of Mexico is primarily diatonic with influences, obvious in folk music, from Africa. Harmonic progressions have been adopted from European harmonic traditions and are observable in accompaniments of Mexican song.

V. Australia

Introductory Remarks:

Australia's first music was that of the Aborigines. As Europe began its colonization, this native music declined. In the twentieth century it was revived as Aboriginal folk music, often mixed with more modern influences. More recently, aboriginal music has become a vehicle of protest concerning Aboriginal issues such as civil rights and land ownership. Today, the most popular music in Australia is that of this revived indigenous music with modern characteristics.

🌐 **Key Word Associations for Australia:** *Dreamtime*, **songmen, Bunggul, Kun-borrk (or Gunborg), Wangga (also Wongga),** (instruments: **didgeridoo (didjeridu), bullroarer, gumleaf)**

General Musical Characteristics:

1. The aboriginal belief in a period in antiquity called *Dreamtime*, is the culture's most poignant demonstration of its belief in the importance of music. Mythology teaches that totemic spirits came to Australia and sung the names of plants, animals, and other natural features. This sung creation, of sorts, brought the country into being. So, music breathed life into the country. Thus, the importance of music in aboriginal culture cannot be overstated.

2. The cultures are based on oral traditions of written stories, song texts, and music. Musical notation is not part of the culture.

3. Music is learned informally through participation and passed on in the community.

4. A typical performance will include a lead singer (songman), optional additional singers   (each with a pair of percussive sticks) and a person playing the **didgeridoo** (didjeridu).

5. Only a few men are recognized as singers. They are called "songmen". They are skilled in improvisation of word and melody and in the presentation of rhythmic patterns, which are at times polyrhythmic.

6. *Clan songs* are songs that are shared among groups of people and passed on from generation to generation with updates added concerning current culture.

7. *Bunggul* is one of three primary styles of music. It is known for its intense texts, which are often epic narrations that continue to be recited (similar to monophonic recitative) after the instrumental accompaniment has ended.

8. *Kun-borrk* (or Gunborg) is another style of music that features stops in the music by the tutti group. These songs usually start with the didgeridoo, to which are added sticks and then the singers.

9. *Wangga* (or Wongga) is the third style of music. This music features a long, high sung pitch at the beginning of a song, followed by the beating of sticks and the playing of the didgeridoo accompanying the song.

Instruments Used:

Different tribes in Australia use various instruments including sticks, boomerangs, clubs, drums and rattles. Additionally, hand clapping and thigh slapping are common.[21]

1. **Didgeridoo (also didjeridu)**: a wind instrument made out of bamboo or eucalyptus that is loud enough to be heard over long distances. It is a little over four feet long and is perhaps the world's oldest instrument. It is considered the national instrument of the Aborigines.

2. **Bullroarer**: the instrument's true name is considered secret and sacred and is not shared with non-Aboriginal people. It is a single wooden slat, about 12-14 inches long and about 2.5 inches wide, that is whirled around in a circle on the end of a rope. It generates a pitch, close to 80Hz (between a B-flat and a B, in the lower range of pitches. (Audible frequencies are, on average, between 20 Hz and 25,000Hz). As the player moves the instrument in height and speed, the pitch varies.

3. **Clapsticks** are percussive instruments that are used in most music. Typically the sticks are made of hardwood and average seven or eight inches in length. One stick is held in each hand and the sticks are struck together near the middle of each stick.

4. **Conch shell**: a large shell into which one blows creating a pitch.

5. **Gumleaf**: The gumleaf is a leaf from a Eucalyptus tree that is commonly found in Australia. The leaf is held against the lower lip and stretched between two hands. The player blows air through the leaf to create a sound. (Many Western children create this effect with blades of grass.)

Tonal System:

Like much of African music, Aboriginal music is not based on a system of standardized pitch. There are no Western instruments to give the singers a precise tonal center of diatonic stability. On the other hand, Western music is prevalent in the cities and places that have come under European influence. Australia is a country operating within ancient and modern traditions simultaneously.

---

[21]This website was created by Aborigines: http://aboriginalart.com.au/didgeridoo/ instruments.html

Chapter 6

❦

A Quick Look at Jazz History

This chapter will attempt to present the reader with various styles of jazz as they appeared in America.[1] Its roots are in West African music (including call-and-response singing) and, in 19th-century African-American ceremonial and work songs. The following outline form will serve as an easy reference for the most basic information.

Its Beginnings

There are conflicting reports as to the actual beginning of *Jazz*. In fact, there even is not agreement among the scholarly community on the actual definition of the term. There are some discussions that date the beginning of jazz around 1917 when the term *Jazz* appeared in Chicago replacing the earlier distinction, *Jass*.[2] This music was Dixieland, or New Orleans Jazz. On the other hand, some say that jazz was born sometime around 1895 in New Orleans when it combined elements of ragtime, blues, and marching band music.[3] Edward Berlin believes that ragtime is most likely the first American music. The first ragtime composition, "My Coal Black Lady," published in 1896, began a widespread fascination with the style until about 1917.[4] It was not only ragtime that was popular in America. The blues was a style born out of tales of emotion found among Black American musicians. Jeff Todd Titon asks questions to which we all want answers: "Is blues a part of jazz?" "Did the stream of blues flow into the river of jazz?"[5] Titon concludes that blues and jazz move historically more parallel than they do chronologically. When the Czech composer Antonin Dvorak arrived in America in 1892, prompted by an invitation to lead the National Conservatory of Music in New York, he offered his opinion in an interview with the New York Herald and said that the future music of America "must be founded upon what are called negro melodies . . . . There is nothing in the whole range of composition that cannot be supplied with themes from this source."[6] Obviously, there were sorts of music that were popular in the early 1890s that an outsider viewed as

---

[1] There are obvious historical links to Africa and the people who were forced into slavery and brought to America. For a summary of these events, see Bob Yurochko's *A Short History of Jazz*, Nelson-Hall Publishers, Chicago, 1993.

[2] Yurochko, *A Short History of Jazz*, p. 28.

[3] http://www.redhotjazz.com/ accessed March 14, 2006.

[4] http://www.edwardaberlin.com/ (See his numerous books on the topic as well.)

[5] Titon, *Worlds of Music*, p. 131.

[6] This website has a archived collection of newspaper articles relevant to Dvorak and America. http://homepage.mac.com/rswinter/DirectTestimony/home.html

interesting and original. These styles were America's new music that eventually led up to the more inclusive term, *Jazz*. What follows, is a summary list of these styles.

I. Ragtime: 1890s+

Although Scott Joplin is considered to be the King of Ragtime, he did not invent the style. The first ragtime song to be published ("My Coal Black Lady," 1896) was by William H. Krell (1873-1933), a white Chicago bandleader. Then, in 1897, he published an instrumental work called "Mississippi Rag" which featured the word *Rag-time* on its cover, the first time that the word appeared in print. But, Krell did not invent ragtime either. The style seems to have emerged primarily in Chicago, St. Louis, and Louisville, Kentucky. Ben Harney (1871-1938), a white songwriter from Louisville, was the first pianist to achieve fame as "The Ragtime Piano Player." He published his *Ben Harney's Rag-time Instructor* in 1897 which described how to *rag*

by improvising syncopations into popular tunes. Ragtime was a march-like music played with syncopations that created an uneven feeling in the "march". Hence, the music is "ragged".[7] Ragtime composers and performers include, **Scott Joplin, James Scott, Joseph Lamb**, Artie Matthews, May Aufderheide, Eubie Blake, Zez Confrey, **Ben Harney**, George Botsford, Charles L. Johnson, Luckey Roberts, Paul Sarebresole, Tom Turpin, and Wilber Sweatman.

II. Blues: 1890s+

The origins of the blues are rather obscure.[8] Black Americans in the rural south sang laments and work songs in a style that eventually became the blues sometime between 1870 and 1900. The songs were often slow and mournful, and although we believe that the songs were originally sung without accompaniment, the guitar and banjo became favored instruments to accompany the singing. In 1912, three blues songs were published, one of which was William C. Handy's (1873-1958), "Memphis Blues". Handy promoted himself as the "Father of the Blues", but scholars agree that his style does not represent the true nature of the style. The sheet music industry took up publication of this style as well as ragtime.

One of the characteristic traits of a blues song is a slight lowering of the third, seventh, and sometimes fifth scale degrees. We refer to this as a blues scale, one in which the pitches are altered. There is a great deal of syncopation and the singer seldom begins on a downbeat or any strong beat for that matter. In fact, the meter and rhythm also seem altered. A blues text begins with a pair of identical rhyming lines followed by a third line of text that answers to the "trouble" presented in the first pair of lines. The texts mostly concern love, hardship, and disappointment. The 12-bar blues pattern refers to a setting of four measures for each line of poetry and a general harmonic pattern of:

---

[7] http://www.edwardaberlin.com/
[8] A nice article with general information is at: http://en.wikipedia.org/wiki/Blues

First line of text:	**tonic**
Second line of text:	**subdominant to tonic**
Third line of text:	**dominant to tonic**

This early blues style evolved into more complex styles and genres that have created the foundation for American popular music. There are different types of blues such as, Country Blues (uses a slide guitar), Delta Blues (often accompanied by slide guitar and harmonica), Piedmont Blues (utilizes a finger-picking technique on the guitar), Memphis Blues (popular in the 1920s-30s; utilized a variety of unusual instruments such as a washboard or mandolin), Jump Blues (uses driving rhythms, shouts, and a saxophone predominantly), Urban Blues, Chicago Blues, and Electric Blues, among others. Boogie-woogie is also a type of blues, popular in the 1940s, that featured piano playing based on an ostinato. Most research concludes that the blues formed the foundation of the rock & roll of the 1960s and eventually rhythm & blues.

Famous blues musicians include, **Bessie Smith**, **B. B. King**, **Muddy Waters**, Joe Oliver (King Oliver), **Billie Holiday**, Buddy Guy, Howlin' Wolf, Blind Blake (Blake Alphonso Higgs), **Ma Rainey**, **Mamie Smith**, Bo Diddley, and John Lee Hooker.[9]

III. Dixieland (New Orleans Jazz): 1900+

Dixieland is a type of jazz that developed in New Orleans in the early 1900s and is sometimes called, New Orleans Jazz. By the 1910s, New Orleans Dixieland bands had taken the style to Chicago and New York City. Some sources credit it as being the first true type of jazz. It apparently was the first type of music before 1917 to be called "jazz", but spelled, "jass".

The musical style is based on simultaneous improvisation resulting in polyphony played by a trumpet, trombone, and clarinet. Underneath the musical lines of the three soloists, whose simultaneous improvisations give this style its recognizable characteristic, is a rhythm section consisting of a drum set, a double bass, a piano, and a guitar or banjo. In 1917, the band named, *Original Dixieland Jass Band*, recorded a hit record, catapulting the style into the mainstream of popularity. Louis Armstrong and his band the *All-Stars* are most often identified with Dixieland Jazz.

In the 1940s, the Dixieland style of improvisation fell out of favor among the public when bebop became popular.

Famous Dixieland musicians include **Louis Armstrong**, Tony Almerico, Turk Murphy, Al Hirt, Pete Fountain, Kenny Ball, Jim Cullum, Tim Laughlin, Eddie Condon, and the band, Dikes of Dixieland of the Assunto family.

---

[9] For an incredibly long list of musicians see: http://en.wikipedia.org/wiki/List_of_blues_musicians

IV. Swing (Swing Jazz and Big Band)

The Swing Era: 1935-45[10]

Swing developed as a style of jazz in the 1920s and 30s. Its feature characteristic is a strong rhythm section of drums and a double bass that propels the rather fast tempo to a distinctive swing time rhythm. Strings of eighth notes become dotted eighth notes and the rhythm seems to "swing". The bands that played this subgenre of jazz tended to be bigger, creating a need for band leaders who would make arrangements for their bands of 15 or so players. Because these groups were larger, the style was sometimes called *Big Band*. Typically, soloists would improvise one at a time, although there were exceptions. A type of accompanying dance, *swing dance*, emerged in the Black American community. The music could be very loud and energetic, creating a rowdy atmosphere. The aggressive music threatened governments in the Soviet Union and in Nazi Germany and swing jazz was banned there.

Famous swing musicians include **Duke Ellington**, **Count Basie**, **Benny Goodman**, **Artie Shaw**, **Gene Krupa**, **Glenn Miller**, **Fletcher Henderson**, **Paul Whiteman**, Jean Goldkette, Chick Webb, Louis Armstrong, Roy Eldridge, Harry Edison, Earl Hines, Art Tatum, Teddy Wilson, and Jelly Roll Morton.

V. Bebop Era: 1945-55

Bebop appeared in the late 1940s (later called bop) as an alternative style for the youthful audience. It was considered the new "cool" jazz. Many of these new cool tunes were actually based on chord progressions of already popular songs. This became such a fashion that these entirely new compositions based on existing chord progressions were given a name: *contrafacts*. (The older song from 1930, "I Got Rhythm" by George Gershwin was a favorite of many songwriters, calling the chord progressions, *rhythm changes*.)

Bebop is characterized by a flatted fifth (the tri-tone) in the diatonic scale and by upper chord tones such as ninths, elevenths, and thirteenths. These altered chords led to a more complex system of bebop scales (or modes), which appeared more modern to audiences. Improvisation played the most important role, (even drummers had solos), challenging the performers with more complex chords. The band typically included a bass, drums, piano, and two solo instruments such as a trumpet or saxophone.

Bebop musicians include **Dizzy Gillespie**, **Charlie Parker**, **Thelonious Monk**, **Bud Powell**, **Max Roach**, **Charles Mingus**, **Stan Getz**, and **Eddie Lockjaw Davis**.

---

[10] Yurochko gives the style an era with these dates. Dates differ according to source.

VI. Rhythm & Blues (R & B): 1940s+

In the 1940s Black American musicians were performing an upbeat popular sort of music that combined elements of jazz and the blues. Previously, it had been referred to as *race music*, which was rather offensive. Jerry Wexler, an influential music producer who later helped promote soul music in the 1960s, coined the term *rhythm and blues* in *Billboard* magazine to replace the older name for this stylish music. This style eventually developed into rock & roll. By the 1970s the term rhythm & blues was more inclusive and referred to a broad spectrum of funk and soul.

Originally, rhythm & blues drew influences from jump music and black gospel songs. (Hard bop results from a combination of styles including rhythm & blues, blues, bebop, and gospel music.) Some of the first rock & roll songs were in the rhythm & blues style, such as, "Shake, rattle and Roll".

At this point, musicians were not concerned with stylistic labels placed on their music. Many musicians who previously had recorded jazz, bebop, or swing, now also recorded rhythm & blues.

Famous rhythm and blues musicians include Fats Domino, Count Basie, Tadd Dameron, Charlie Mingus, "Big Mama" Thornton, Lionel Hampton, Eddie "Cleanhead" Vinson, Professor Longhair, Clarence "Frogman" Henry, Frankie Ford, Irma Thomas, The Neville Brothers, and Dr. John.

VII. Hard Bop: 1950s

In the 1950s Hard Bop developed out of bebop. The tempo of Hard Bop could be slower and the music was more appealing to a wider audience not versed in contemporary music. It incorporated influences from blues, rhythm and blues, and gospel music focusing on the playing of the saxophone and the piano.

Hard Bop musicians include **Canonball Adderley**, **Thelonious Monk**, **Hank Mobley**, Charles Mingus, **Sonny Rollins**, Art Blakey, Clifford Brown, Sonny Clark, **John Coltrane**, **Miles Davis,** Benny Golson, Dexter Gordon, Joe Henderson, Blue Mitchell, Lee Morgan, and Tadd Dameron, among others.

VIII. Rock & Roll: 1950+

Rock & roll emerged in the 1950s in the Southern United States and spread quickly across the nation and then throughout the Western world. Eventually, it was referred to as *rock*. Originally, rock & roll combined influences from boogie-woogie, jazz, blues, and rhythm & blues. In addition to these popular styles, rock & roll was influenced in the south by Appalachian folk music, gospel, and country and western music.[11] In Cleveland, Ohio, in 1951, it was the radio disc jockey Alan Freed who first played this mostly Black American music for his white audiences. Freed is credited with first using the term *rock & roll* to describe this new invigorating sort of rhythm & blues music.

Experts do not agree wholly about which song should be designated as the first rock & roll record. These records should be considered among the first: "Rocket 88" (1951) by Jackie Brenston & His Delta Cats, "Maybelline" and "Johnny B. Goode" by Chuck Berry, and "Rock Around the Clock" by Bill Haley & His Comets. Other important musicians in this new style include **Elvis Presley**, **Fats Domino**, **Little Richard**, and **Jerry Lee Lewis**.

IX. Conclusion

Following the birth of rock & roll, American popular music took many paths. Jazz remained popular in many forms. Country music fused with other styles. The electronic age of instruments (and composition!) has taken popular music into unimaginable new avenues. Several attempts are being made even now to discuss and classify this phenomenal time in music's history. Never before has the Western world seen such a variety of styles within one seemingly, united country (despite our melting pot attributes). Alongside the music born out of academia and its composers is a wealth of music born out of popular culture, amateur and professional. New media outlets for music are being added to our music culture, such as music for video games, other gaming systems, and even cell phones. The future of art music and the future of popular music are surely interesting topics for contemplation. Will popular music replace classical art music? Will classical art music experience a complete fusion with popular music? Will a chasm emerge between the museum art music of the past and the art music of the future? Future generations will have decisions to make and distinctions to clarify.

---

[11]The article at http://en.wikipedia.org/wiki/Rock_and_roll gives a nice summary of the early uses of the term "rock" as well as the origins of the style.

Chapter 7

ℭℜ

Famous Pieces of Music Literature

<u>Listed by Composer</u>

Adams, John (b. 1947)

Nixon in China (opera, 1987)
Phrygian Gates, 1977
Shaker Loops, 1978
Short Ride in a Fast Machine, 1986

Bach, Carl Philipp Emanuel (1714-88)

Clavier-Sonaten für Kenner und
    Liebhaber, 1779-83
On Playing the Keyboard, (treatise), 1753

Bach, Johann Sebastian (1685-1750)

Brandenburg Concerti, 1721
Art of Fugue, BWV 1080, (before
    1742, revised 1748-49)
Christ lag in Todes Banden, BWV 4
    (*Christ lay in bonds of death*), Cantata,
    1708
Christmas Oratorio, BWV 248, 1734-35
Coffee Cantata, BWV 211, ca. 1734-35
Das wohltemperirte Clavier (*The Well-*
    Tempered Keyboard) 1722, 1740
Goldberg Variations, BWV 988, 1741-42
Magnificat, BWV 243, ca. 1732-35
Mass in B Minor, 1747-49
Musikalisches Opfer (*A Musical Offering*),
    BWV 1079, 1747
Peasant Cantata, BWV 212, 1742
St. John Passion, BWV 245, 1724
St. Matthew Passion, BWV 244, 1727
Wachet auf, ruft uns die Stimme
    (*"Wakeup," the voice calls to us*), BWV
    140, Cantata, 1731

Barber, Samuel (1910-1981)

Adagio for Strings, 1936
Antony and Cleopatra, opera, 1966
Dover Beach (baritone and string
    quartet), 1931)
Knoxville, Summer of 1915, 1947

Barron, Louis (1920-89) and Bebe
    Barron (b. 1926)

Forbidden Planet, 1956

Bartok, Béla (1881-1945)

Concerto for Orchestra, 1943
Music for Strings, Percussion, and
    Celesta, 1936

Beach, Amy Marcy Cheney (1867-1944)

Gaelic Symphony, 1896

Beethoven, Ludwig van (1770-1827)

Appassionata Sonata, 1804
Christus am Ölberge, 1803
Diabelli Variations, 1819; 1822-23
Emperor's Piano Concerto, 1809
Eroica Symphony (No. 3), 1803
Fidelio, 1814
Kreutzer Violin Sonata, Op. 47, 1802-03
Leonore Overture, 1815
Missa solemnis in D Major, 1819-23
Moonlight Sonata, Op. 27/2, 1801
Pathëtique Sonata, Op. 13, 1797-98
Symphonie pastorale (No. 6), 1807-8
Symphony No. 5 in C Minor, Op. 67,
    1807-08
Symphony No. 9 (the "choral symphony"
    in D Minor, Op. 125, (1822-24)
Tempest Sonata, Op. 31/2, 1802
Waldstein Sonata, Op. 53, 1803-04

Bellini, Vincenzo (1801-35)

Norma, 1831

Berg, Alban (1885-1935)

Lulu, 1937
Wozzeck, 1925

Berlioz, Hector (1803-69)

Harold en Italie, (program symphony),
    1834
La damnation de Faust, (secular
    oratorio), 1846
L'enfance du Christ, (sacred trilogy) 1854
Roman Carnival Overture, 1844
Roméo et Juliette, (program symphony),
    1839
Symphonie fantastique, (program
    symphony), 1830
Traité de l'instrmentation (treatise), 1843

Bernstein, Leonard (1918-90)

Candide, 1956
Chichester Psalms, 1965
Jeremiah Symphony (No. 1, 1942)
Kaddish Symphony (No. 3, 1963)
On The Town (Three Dance Episodes, 1945)
West Side Story, 1957

Bingen, Hildegard von (1098-1179)

Ordo Virtutum, 1152

Bizet, Georges (1838-75)

Carmen, 1873-75

Brahms, Johannes (1833-97)

Academic Festival Overture, 1880
Ein deutsches Requiem (A German Requiem, 1857-1868)
Tragic Overture, 1880
Variations on a Theme by Haydn, Op. 56, 1873

Britten, Benjamin (1913-76)

Peter Grimes (opera, 1945)
War Requiem, 1962
Ceremony of Carols, 1942

Caccini, Giulio (1551-1618)

Le nuove musiche, 1602

Cage, John (1912-92)

Sonatas and Interludes, 1946-48
4'33", 1952
Music of Changes, 1951

Chopin, Frédéric (1810-1849)

Sonata No. 2 in B-flat Minor, 1839
24 Preludes, Op. 28, 1838-39
12 Etudes, Op. 10, 1829-1833

Copland, Aaron (1900-90)

Appalachian Spring, 1944
Billy the Kid, 1938
Fanfare for the Common Man, 1942
Rodeo, 1942

Corigliano, John (b. 1938)

The Ghosts of Versailles, 1987

Couperin, François (1668-1733)

Les Nations (trio sonatas, pub. 1726)

Crumb, George (b. 1929)

Ancient Voices of Children, 1970
Black Angels: 13 Images from the Dark Land, 1970

Debussy, Claude (1862-1918)

Afternoon of a Faun (Prélude à L'après-midi d'un faune, 1894)
La Mer (*The Sea*, tone poem, 1903-05)
Pelléas et Mélisande, (opera, 1902)

Donizetti, Gaetano (1797-1848)

Don Pasquale, 1843
L'elisir d'amore (*The Elixir of Love*, 1832)
Lucia di Lammermoor, 1835
Mary Stuarda (*Mary Queen of Scots*, 1832)

Dvořák, Antonín (1841-1904)

New World Symphony, 1893

Elgar, Edward (1857-1934)

Enigma Variations, 1899
Pomp and Circumstance march, ca. 1901

Falla, Manuel de (1876-1946)

Nights in the Gardens of Spain, 1909-15

Floyd, Carlisle (b. 1926)

Susannah, 1955

Gabrieli, Giovanni (ca. 1557-1612)

In ecclesiis, pub. 1615
Sacrae symphoniae, vol I, 1597; vol II, 1615

Gay, John (1685-1732)

A Beggar's Opera, 1728

Gershwin, George (1898-1937)

American in Paris, 1928
Concerto in F, 1925
Porgy and Bess, 1935
Rhapsody in Blue, 1924

Glass, Philip (b. 1937)

Einstein on the Beach, 1975-76
Glassworks, 1981

Gluck, Christoph Willibald (1714-87)

Alceste, 1767
Iphigénie en Aulide, 1774
Orfeo ed Euridice, 1762

Gounod, Charles (1818-93)

Faust, 1859

Grieg, Edvard (1843-1907)

Peer Gynt Suite, 1875

Händel, Georg Friedrich (1685-1759) *Giulio Cesare* (opera, 1724)
Messiah (oratorio, 1742)
Rinaldo (opera, 1711)
Water Music, 1717

Haydn, Franz Joseph (1732-1809)

The Creation, 1796-98
Emperor Quartet (String Quartet
in C Major, Op. 76, No. 3, 1797)
London Symphonies (Nos. 93-104),
1791-95
Oxford Symphony, 1789
Surprise Symphony (No. 94), 1791

Hindemith, Paul (1895-1963)

Mathis der Maler, 1933-35

Holst, Gustav (1874-1934)

The Planets, 1914-16

Humperdinck, Engelbert (1854-1921)

Hänsel und Gretel, 1893

Ives, Charles (1874-1954)

The Concord Sonata, (Piano Sonata No. 2,
1910-15)
Three Places in New England, 1911-17
The Unanswered Question, 1908
114 Songs, pub. 1922
Variations on America, 1892

Joplin, Scott (1868-1917)

The Entertainer, 1902
Gladioulus Rag, 1907
Maple Leaf Rag, 1899
Treemonisha, 1911

Josquin des Prez (ca. 1450-1521)

Missa Pange lingua, ca. 1514, pub. 1539

Kodály, Zoltán (1882-1967)

Háry János, (Singspiel, 1925-27)

Leoncavallo, Ruggiero (1858-1919)

Pagliacci (*The Clowns*), 1892

Léonin (fl. 1163-90)

Magnus liber organi, 13th c.

Liszt, Franz (1811-1886)

Faust Symphony, 1857

Les Préludes, ca. 1853

Transcendental Etudes, I, 1839

Machaut, Guillaume de (ca. 1300-77)

Messe de Notre Dame (*Mass of Notre Dame*), early 1360s

Mahler, Gustav (1860-1911)

Kindertotenlieder, 1901-04
Das Lied von der Erde, 1908
Resurrection Symphony (No. 2 in C Minor, 1888-94/1903)
Titan Symphony (No. 1 in D Major, 1884-1888, rev.1893-6)

Massenet, Jules (1842-1912)

Manon (opera, 1884)

Mendelssohn, Felix (1809-47)

Elijah, (oratorio, 1846)
Italian Symphony (No. 4). 1833
Overture to *A Midsummer Night's Dream* Op.21, 1826
Reformation Symphony (No. 5 in D Minor, Op. 107, 1830)
Scottish Symphony (No. 3 in A Minor, Op. 56, 1842)
Songs Without Words, 1829-45

Menotti, Gian Carlo (b. 1911)

Amahl and the Night Visitors, 1951
The Consul, 1949
The Telephone, opera, 1946

Messiaen, Olivier (1908-92)
of

Quatuor pour la fin du temps (*Quartet for the end time*), 1940-41

Monteverdi, Claudio (1567-1643)*Il*

Combattimento di Tancredi e Clorinda (madrigals), 1624
Il ritorno d'Ulisse (*The Return of Ulysses*), 1639-41
L'incoronazione di Poppea (*The Coronation of Poppea*), 1642
L'Orfeo, 1607

Mozart, Wolfgang Amadeus (1756-91)

Cosi fan tutte, 1790
Die Entführung aus dem Serail, 1782
Die Zauberflöte, 1791
Don Giovanni, 1787
Haffner Symphony, 1782
Jupiter Symphony, 1788
Le Nozze di Figaro, 1786
Requiem, 1791

Musorgsky, Modest (1839-1881)

Boris Godunov, 1868-69
Pictures at an Exhibition, 1874

Orff, Carl (1895-1982)

Carmina burana, 1936

Palestrina, Giovanni Pierluigi da
    (ca. 1525/26-94)

Pope Marcellus Mass, 1567

Penderecki, Krzysztof (b. 1933)

Threnody for the Victims of Hiroshima,
    1960

Pergolesi, Giovanni Battista (1710-36)

La serva padrona (intermezzi), 1733
Stabat Mater, 1736

Peri, Jacopo (1561-1633)

Euridice, (our first surviving opera, 1600)

Prokofiev, Sergei (1891-1953)

Alexander Nevsky, 1938
Peter and the Wolf, 1936

Puccini, Giacomo (1858-1924)

La boheme, 1896
Tosca, 1900

Purcell, Henry (1659-95)

Dido and Aeneas, 1689

Quantz, Johann Joachim (1697-1773)

On Playing the Flute, (book), 1752

Rameau, Jean-Puilippe (1683-1764)

Castor et Pollux (*Castor and Pollux*),
    1737
Les Indes galantes (*The Gallant Indies*),
    1735
Traité de l'harmonie (*Treatise on
    Harmony*), 1722

Ravel, Maurice (1875-1937)

Bolero, 1928
Daphnis et Chloé (1st and 2nd suites), 1912

Respighi, Ottorino (1879-1936)

Pines of Rome, 1924

Riley, Terry (b. 1935)

In C, 1964

Rimsky-Korsakov, Nikolay (1844-1908)

Scheherazade, Op. 35, 1888

Rossini, Gioachino (1792-1868)

Guillaume Tell (*William Tell*, 1829)
Il Barbiere di Siviglia (The Barber of
    Seville, 1816)

Saint-Saëns, Camille (1835-1921)

Carnival of the Animals, 1886

Schoenberg, Arnold (1874-1951)

Harmonielehre, (treatise, 1910-11)
Pierrot Lunaire, 1912
Variationen für Orchester, 1926
Verklärte Nacht, 1899/1917

Schubert, Franz (1797-1828)

Erlkönig, 1815
Gretchen am Spinnrade, 1814
Trout Quintet, (Piano quintet in A Major,
      D667, 1819)
The Unfinished Symphony (No. 8, 1822)
Wanderer Fantasy (piano, 1822)
Winterreise (song cycle, 1827)

Schumann, Robert (1810-1856)

Carnaval (solo piano, 1833-35)
Rhenish Symphony (No. 3 in E-flat Major,
      Op. 97, 1850)

Schütz, Heinrich (1585-1672)

The Psalms of David, 1619, 1661

Shostokovich, Dmitry (1906-75)

Lady Macbeth of Mtsensk (opera, 1934)
Leningrad Symphony, written in 1941
      (No. 7 in C Major, Op. 60)

Smetana, Bedrich (1824-84)

The Bartered Bride, 1866
The Moldau, 1874

Sousa, John Philip (1854-1932)

The Stars and Stripes Forever, 1897

Still, William Grant (1895-1978)

Afro-American Symphony, 1930-31

Strauss, Richard (1864-1949)

Also sprach Zarathustra, 1896
Don Juan, 1888-89
Don Quixote, 1897
Ein Heldenleben, 1898
Elektra, 1908
Rosenkavalier, 1911
Salome, 1905
Till Eulenspiegels lustige Streiche, 1895

Stravinisky, Igor (1882-1971)

L' Histoire du soldat, 1918
Firebird, 1910
Petruska, 1911
Rite of Spring, 1913

	The Rake's Progress (opera, 1951)
	Symphony of Psalms, 1930
Tchaikovsky, Pyotr Ilyich (1840-93) (Chaykovsky)	*1812 Festive Overture*, 1880
	The Nutcraker, 1892
	Pathétique Symphony, (No. 6, 1893)
	Romeo and Juliet, 1878
	Sleeping Beauty, 1889
	Swan Lake, 1876
Thomas, Ambroise (1811-1896)	*Mignon*, 1866
Varèse, Edgard (1883-1965)	*Hyperprism*, 1923
	Ionisation, 1929-31
	Poème electronique, 1956-58
Vaughan Williams Ralph (1872-1958)	*A Sea Symphony*, 1903-09
	Fantasia on a Theme by Thomas Tallis, 1910
Verdi, Giuseppe (1813-1901)	*Aida,* 1871
	Falstaff, 1893
	Il Trovatore, 1853
	La forza de destino, 1862
	La Traviata, 1853
	Luisa Miller, 1849
	Messa di Requiem, 1874
	Otello, 1887
	Rigoletto, 1851
Vitry, Philippe de (ca. 1291-1361)	*Ars nova* (treatise from ca. 1323)
Vivaldi, Antonio (1678-1741)	*Le quattro stagioni* (*The Four Seasons*), pub. ca. 1725
Wagner, Richard (1813-83)	*Lohengrin,* 1850
	Der Ring des Nibelungen (completed 1876)
	Siegfried, 1876
	Tristan und Isolde, 1865
Weber, Carl Maria von (1786-1826)	*Der Freischütz,* 1821
Webern, Anton (1883-1945)	Symphony, Op. 21, 1929
Weill, Kurt (1900-50)	*Threepenny Opera,* 1928

Listed by Title

English titles are listed when relevant.

114 Songs, 1922	Ives
1812 Overture, 1880	Tchaikovsky
4'33", 1952	Cage
Abduction from the Seraglio, The 1782	Mozart
Academic Festival Overture, 1880	Brahms
Adagio for Strings, 1936	Barber
Afro-American Symphony, 1930-31	Still
Afternoon of a Faun, 1894	Debussy
Aida, 1871	Verdi
Alceste, 1767	Gluck
Alexander Nevsky, 1938	Prokofiev
Also sprach Zarathustra, 1896	Strauss, R.
Amahl and the Night Visitors, 1951	Menotti
American in Paris, 1928	Gershwin
Ancient Voices of Children, 1970	Crumb
Antony and Cleopatra, opera, 1966	Barber
Appalachian Spring, 1944	Copland
Appassionata Sonata, 1804	Beethoven
Ars nova (treatise), ca. 1323	Vitry
Art of Fugue, The, BWV 1080, 1749-50	J. S. Bach
Barber of Seville, The, 1816	Rossini
Bartered Bride, The, 1866	Smetana
A Beggar's Opera, 1728	Gay
Billy the Kid, 1938	Copland
Black Angels: 13 Images from the Dark Land, 1970	Crumb
Boris Godunov, 1868-69	Musorgsky
Brandenburg Concerti, 1721	J. S. Bach
Candide, 1956	Bernstein
Carmen, 1873-75	Bizet
Carmina burana, 1936	Orff
Carnaval, 1833-35	Schumann, R.
Carnival of the Animals, 1886	Saint-Saëns
Castor et Pollux (Castor and Pollux), 1737	Rameau
Ceremony of Carols, 1942	Britten
Chichester Psalms, 1965	Bernstein
Choral Symphony (No. 9), 1822-24	Beethoven
Christ lag in Todes Banden, BWV 4	J. S. Bach
(Christ lay in bonds of death), Cantata, 1708	
Christmas Oratorio, BWV 248, 1734-35	J. S. Bach
Christus am Ölberge, 1803	Beethoven
Clavier-Sonaten für Kenner und Liebhaber, 1779-83	C. P. E. Bach

Coffee Cantata, BWV 211, ca. 1734-35	J. S. Bach
Concerto for Orchestra, 1943	Bartok
Concerto in F, 1925	Gershwin
Concord Sonata, 1910-15	Ives
Consul, The, 1949	Menotti
Cosi fan tutte, 1790	Mozart
Creation, The, 1796-98	Haydn
Daphnis et Chloé (1st and 2nd suites), 1912	Ravel
Das Lied von der Erde, 1908	Mahler
Das wohltemperirte Clavier (*The Well-Tempered Keyboard*) 1722, 1740	J. S. Bach
Der Freischütz, 1821	Weber
Der Ring des Nibelungen, 1876	Wagner
Diabelli Variations, 1819; 1822-23	Beethoven
Dido and Aeneas, 1689	Purcell
Die Entführung aus dem Serail, 1782	Mozart
Die Zauberflöte, 1791	Mozart
Don Giovanni, 1787	Mozart
Don Juan, 1888-89	R. Strauss
Don Pasquale, 1843	Donizetti
Dover Beach (baritone and string quartet), 1931	Barber
Ein deutsches Requiem, 1857-68	Brahms
Ein Heldenleben, 1898	Strauss, R.
Einstein on the Beach, 1975	Glass
Elektra, 1908	Strauss, R.
Elijah, 1846	Mendelssohn
Elixir of Love, The, 1832	Donizetti
Emperor's Piano Concerto, 1809	Beethoven
Enigma Variations, 1899	Elgar
Entertainer, The, 1902	Joplin
Erlkönig, 1815	Schubert
Eroica Symphony (No. 3), 1803	Beethoven
Euridice, 1600	Peri
Falstaff, 1893	Verdi
Fanfare for the Common Man, 1942	Copland
Fantasia on a Theme by Thomas Tallis, 1910	Vaughan Williams
Faust Symphony, 1857	Liszt
Faust, 1859	Gounod
Fidelio, 1814	Beethoven
Firebird, 1910	Stravinsky
Forbidden Planet, 1956	Barron and Barron
Gaelic Symphony, 1896	Beach
German Requiem, A, 1857-68	Brahms
Ghosts of Versailles, The, 1987	Corigliano
Giulio Cesare (opera), 1724	Händel

Gladioulus Rag, 1907	Joplin
Glassworks, 1981	Glass
Goldberg Variations, BWV 988, 1741-42	J. S. Bach
Gretchen am Spinnrade, 1814	Schubert
Guillaume Tell, 1829	Rossini
Haffner Symphony, 1782	Mozart
Hänsel und Gretel, 1893	Humperdinck
Harmonielehre, 1910-11	Schoenberg
Harold en Italie, (program symphony), 1834	Berlioz
Háry János, 1925-27	Kodaly
Hyperprism, 1923	Varèse
Il Barbiere di Siviglia, 1816	Rossini
Il Combattimento di Tancredi e Clorinda (madrigals), 1624	Monteverdi
Il ritorno d'Ulisse (*The Return of Ulysses*), 1639-41	Monteverdi
Il Trovatore, 1853	Verdi
In C, 1964	Riley
In ecclesiis, pub. 1615	G. Gabrieli
Ionisation, 1929-31	Varese
Iphigénie en Aulide, 1774	Gluck
Italian Symphony, 1833	Mendelssohn
Jeremiah Symphony, 1942	Bernstein
Jupiter Symphony, 1788	Mozart
Kaddish Symphony, 1963	Bernstein
Kindertotenlieder, 1910-04	Mahler
Knoxville, Summer of 1915, 1947	Barber
Kreutzer Sonata, 1803	Beethoven
L'elisir d'amore, 1832	Donizetti
L'enfance du Christ, (sacred trilogy) 1854	Berlioz
L'Histoire du soldat, 1918	Stravinsky
L'incoronazione di Poppea (*The Coronation of Poppea*), 1642	Monteverdi
L'Orfeo, 1607	Monteverdi
La boheme, 1896	Puccini
La damnation de Faust, (secular oratorio), 1846	Berlioz
La forza de destino, 1862	Verdi
La mer, 1903-05	Debussy
La serva padrona, 1733	Pergolesi
La Traviata, 1853	Verdi
Lady Macbeth of Mtsensk, 1934	Shostokovich
Le Nozze di Figaro, 1786	Mozart
Le nuove musiche, 1602	Caccini
Le quattro stagioni (*The Four Seasons*), pub. ca. 1725	Vivaldi
Leningrad Symphony, 1941	Shostokovich
Leonore Overture, 1815	Beethoven
Les Indes galantes (*The Gallant Indies*), 1735	Rameau
Les Nations, 1726	Couperin

Les Préludes, ca. 1853	Liszt
Lohengrin, 1850	Wagner
London Symphonies, 1791-95	Haydn
Lucia di Lammermoor, 1835	Donizetti
Luisa Miller, 1849	Verdi
Lulu, 1937	Berg
Magic Flute. The, 1791	Mozart
Magnus liber organi, 13th c.	Léonin
Manon, 1884	Massenet
Maple Leaf Rag, 1899	Joplin
Marriage of Figaro, The, 1786	Mozart
Mary Queen of Scots, 1832	Donizetti
Mary Stuarda, (*Mary Queen of Scots*), 1832	Donizetti
Mass in B Minor, 1747-49	J. S. Bach
Mathis der Maler, 1933-35	Hindemith
Messe de Notre Dame (*Mass of Notre Dame*), early 1360s	Machaut
Messiah (oratorio), 1742	Händel
Mignon, 1866	Thomas
Missa Pange lingua, pub. 1539	Josquin
Missa solemnis in D Major, 1819-23	Beethoven
Moldau, The, 1874	Smetana
Music for Strings, Percussion, and Celesta, 1936	Bartok
Musical Offering, A, 1747	J. S. Bach
Music of Changes, 1951	Cage
Musikalisches Opfer (*A Musical Offering*), 1747	J. S. Bach
New World Symphony, 1893	Dvorák
Nights in the Gardens of Spain, 1909-15	Falla
Nixon in China, 1987	Adams
Norma, 1831	Bellini
Nutcracker, The, 1892	Tchaikovsky
On Playing the Flute, (book), 1752	Quantz
On Playing the Keyboard, (treatise), 1753	C. P. E. Bach
On The Town, 1945	Bernstein
Ordo Virtutum, 1152	Hildegard
Orfeo ed Euridice, 1762	Gluck
Otello, 1887	Verdi
Overture to A Midsummer Night's Dream, 1826	Mendelssohn
Oxford Symphony, 1789	Haydn
Pagliacci (*The Clowns*), 1892	Leoncavallo
Pastoral Symphony, (*Symphonie pastorale* No. 6), 1807-08	Beethoven
Pathëtique Sonata, Op. 14, 1797-98	Beethoven
Peasant Cantata, BWV 212, 1742	J. S. Bach
Peer Gynt Suite, 1875	Grieg
Pelléas et Mélisande, 1902	Debussy
Peter and the Wolf, 1936	Prokofiev

Peter Grimes, 1945   Britten
Petruska, 1911   Stravinsky
Phrygian Gates, 1977   Adams
Pictures at an Exhibition, 1874   Musorgsky
Pierrot Lunaire, 1912   Schoenberg
Pines of Rome, 1924   Respighi
Planets, The, 1914-16   Holst
Poème electronique, 1956-58   Varèse
Pomp and Circumstance, ca. 1901   Elgar
Pope Marcellus Mass, 1567   Palestrina
Porgy and Bess, 1935   Gershwin
Quatuor pour la fin du temps (Quartet for the end of   Messiaen
    time), 1940-41
Rake's Progress, The, 1951   Stravinsky
Reformation Symphony, 1830   Mendelssohn
Requiem   Berlioz (1837)
                                                          Britten (1962)
                                                          Duruflé (1947)
                                                          Faure (1887)
                                                          Liszt (1867-68)
                                                          Mozart (1791)
                                                          Ockeghem (15th c.;
                                                              our first)
                                                          Verdi (1874)
                                                          Brahms (1857-68)
Resurrection Symphony, 1888-94/1903)   Mahler
Rhapsody in Blue, 1924   Gershwin
Rhenish Symphony, 1850   R. Schumann
Rigoletto, 1851   Verdi
Rinaldo, 1711   Händel
Ring, The (Der Ring des Nibelungen,), 1876   Wagner
Rite of Spring, 1913   Stravinisky
Rodeo, 1942   Copland
Roman Carnival Overture, 1844   Berlioz
Romeo and Juliet, 1878   Tchaikovsky
Roméo et Juliette, (program symphony), 1839   Berlioz
Rosenkavalier, 1911   Strauss, R.
Sacrae symphoniae, vol I, 1597; vol II, 1615   Gabrieli, G.
Salome, 1905   R. Strauss
Scheherazade, 1888   Rimsky-Korsakov
Scottish Symphony, 1842   Mendelssohn
Sea Symphony, A, 1903-09   Vaughan Williams
Shaker Loops, 1978   Adams
Short Ride in a Fast Machine, 1986   Adams
Siegfried, 1876   Wagner

Sleeping Beauty, 1889	Tchaikovsky
Sonatas and Interludes, 1946-48	Cage
Songs Without Words, 1829-45	Mendelssohn
St. John Passion, BWV 245, 1724	J. S. Bach
St. Matthew Passion, BWV 244, 1727	J. S. Bach
Stars and Stripes Forever, The, 1897	Sousa
Surprise Symphony, 1791	Haydn
Susannah, 1955	Floyd
Swan Lake, 1876	Tchaikovsky
Symphonie fantastique, 1830	Berlioz
Symphony, Op. 21, 1929	Webern
Symphony of Psalms, 1930	Stravinsky
Telephone, The, 1947	Menotti
Tempest Sonata, 1802	Beethoven
The Pathétique Symphony (N0. 6), 1893	Tchaikovsky
Three Places in New England, 1911-17	Ives
Threepenny Opera, 1928	Weill
Threnody for the Victims of Hiroshima, 1960	Penderecki
Till Eulenspiegels lustige Streiche, 1895	Strauss, R.
Titan Symphony, 1884-88/1893-96	Mahler
Tosca, 1900	Puccini
Tragic Overture, 1880	Brahms
Traité de l'harmonie (Treatise on Harmony), 1722	Rameau
Traité de l'instrmentation (treatise), 1843	Berlioz
Transcendental Etudes I, 1839	Liszt
Treemonisha, 1911	Joplin
Tristan und Isolde, 1865	Wagner
Trout Quintet, 1819	Schubert
Unanswered Question, The, 1908	Ives
Unfinished Symphony, The, 1822	Schubert
Variationen für Orchester, 1926	Schoenber
Variations on America, 1892	Ives
Variations on a Theme by Haydn, 1873	Brahms
Verklärte Nacht, 1899/1917	Schoenberg
Wachet auf, ruft uns die Stimme ("*Wakeup*," *the voice calls to us*), 1731	J. S. Bach
Waldstein Sonata, 1803-04	Beethoven
Wanderer Fantasy, 1822	Schubert
War Requiem, 1962	Britten
Water Music, 1717	Händel
Well-Tempered Clavier, The, 1722, 1740	J. S. Bach
West Side Story, 1957	Bernstein
William Tell, 1829	Rossini
Winterreise, 1827	Schubert
Wozzeck, 1925	Berg

Chapter 8

ℭ℟

Our Terminology to Review

The following terms are just a few that form the core of our musical language. For specific definitions, I recommend *The New Harvard Dictionary of Music* edited by Don Randel. This dictionary is an invaluable reference that all musicians should have on their bookshelf. The terms below are grouped into categories, sometimes belonging in two or even three categories. The competent musician should be able to explain the nature of each category and discuss the subtle variants in meanings when a term, such as fugue or fugal, appears in more than one category.

Here are a few further points to make:

1. It is important to review when each genre developed. This way you can avoid embarrassing remarks such as, "the symphonies of Handel," the "operas of the Renaissance," or the "tone poems of Beethoven." (I have seen all of these incorrect statements on student exams.)

2. Keep the forms and the genres clearly defined in your mind. Some terms serve dual functions. For instance, a fugue is a genre, but also a form. A string quartet is a genre (a chamber composition in three or four movements), but we also call the performing group of two violins, a viola, and a cello, a string quartet. Typically, string quartets play string quartets. (See how our American usage of the terminology can be annoying?) Make sure you are able to clarify your use of all of our terminology. (To clarify the above statement, one could reword it: "String quartet groups typically play string quartet compositions.")

Genres

Some pieces have a genre and a subgenre. For instance, a piece can be an aria from an opera. Therefore, its larger genre is an opera, and the subgenre is aria.

air
alba
allemande
anthem
antiphon
aria
ballad opera
ballade
ballata
ballet
bourrée
branle
caccia
canon
canso
cantata
canzona
chaccone
chanson
chant
character piece
choral fugue
chorale
chorale prelude
clausula
concerto
concerto grosso
concerto ripieno
conductus
courante
divertimento
etude
fantasia
fauxbourdon
French ouverture
frottola
fugue
galliard
gigue
gradual
grand concerto
hocket
hymn

incidental music
intermedio
intermezzo
Italian overture
lai
Ländler
lauda
Lied
lute song
madrigal
madrigal comedy
march
masque
Mass
mazurka
Meistergesang
melodrama
minnesang
minstrel song
minuet
monody
morality play
motet
music drama
musical
musical play
nocturne
opera
opera buffa
opera comique
opera seria
operetta
oratorio
orchestral Lied
organ prelude
organum
overture
partita
passacaglia
Passion
pasticcio
pastourelle
pavane

piano quartet
piano trio
plainchant
plainsong
prelude
program symphony
quodlibet
recitative
Requiem
ricercare
rondeau
rondellus
rondo
sacred concerto
saltarello
sarabande
sequence
serenade
serenata
sinfonia
Singspiel
sonata
sonata da camera
sonata da chiesa
song
song cycle
string quartet
string trio
suite
symphonic poem
symphony
toccata
tone poem
tragédie lyrique
trio sonata
trope
Troubadour song
Trouvère song
verset
villancico
virelai

Forms[1]

bar form	minuet and trio	sonata-rondo form
binary	modified strophic	sonatina
chaccone	passacaglia	song form
concerto form	ritornello form	strophic
da capo aria form	rondo	ternary
dal segno aria form	scherzo and trio	theme and variations
fugue	sonata form	through-composed

Performing Groups

band	choir	string quartet
basso continuo group	duet	string trio
brass quintet	orchestra	trio sonata
chamber ensemble	piano quartet	woodwind quintet
chamber orchestra	piano trio	

Adjectives that describe a musical style of some sort

accented	electronic	non-metrical
aleatoric	Empfindsamkeit (noun)	orchestral
arioso	English	polymetric
Ars Nova (noun)	expressionistic	polyrhythmic
atonal	French	polytonal
augmented	fugal	programmatic
Baroque	German	recitative-like
cantabile	imitative	Renaissance
chamber	impressionistic	rococo
choral	Italian	romantic
chromatic	liturgical	serial (serialism, noun)
Classic	lyrical	sostenuto (sustained)
consonant	marcato	Sprechstimme (noun)
contemporary	Medieval	staccato (detached)
cyclic	melismatic	syncopated
diatonic	modal	triadic
dissonant	musique concrete (noun)	virtuosic

---

[1]See Chapter 4 for descriptions of the forms.

Textures (nouns, adjectives, adverbs)

contrapuntal texture

fugal texture

heterophony (heterophonic, heterophonically)

homophony (homophonic, homophonically)

homorhythm (homorhythmic)

monophony (monophonic, monophonically)

polyphony (polyphonic, polyphonically)

trio sonata texture

Terms that refer to parts of a particular form or place in the music

answer

cadence

cadential material

cadenza

cantus firmus

coda

codetta

countersubject

da capo

development

episode

exposition

fixed idea

Leitmotif

melisma

motive (motif)

ostinato

period

phrase

recapitulation

refrain

ritornello

solo

subject

theme

trio

Tempos

a tempo (return to preceding tempo)

accelerando (get faster)

adagio (slow, not as slow as largo)

allegro (fast)

andante (walking tempo)

cédez (go slower)

grave (heavy, slow)

L'istesso tempo (in the same tempo)

largando (growing slower)

larghetto (a little slow)

largo (very slow and broad)

lento (slow)

moderato (between allegro and andante)

pressez (go faster)

prestissimo (as fast as possible)

presto (very fast)

rallentando (growing slower and slower)

rallentato (go at a slower pace)

rapido (rapidly)

ritardando (growing slower and slower)

ritenuto (held back)

rubato (robbed, borrowed time)

scherzoso (lightly, jestingly)

stentando (retarding, dragging)

stringendo (hastening)

tardo (lingering, slow)

trattenuto (held back)

vivace (lively, animated)

Dynamics

calandro (decreasing)

crescendo (get louder)

decrescendo (get softer)

diminuendo (diminishing in loudness)

forte (loud)

fortissimo (very loud)

mezzo forte (half, moderately loud)

mezzo piano (half, moderately soft)

morendo (dying away)

perdendosi (dying away)

pianissimo (very soft)

piano (soft)

rinforzato (sudden, louder emphasis)

sforzando (sudden stress or emphasis)

<u>Descriptive terms for the tempos, dynamics, and style</u>

assai (very)

avec (with)

bewegt (moved, agitated)

breve (short)

brillante (showy)

brio (fire)

cantabile (singing)

chiuso (closed, humming)

come prima (as before)

con (with)

corto (short)

desto (sprightly)

deux (two)

divisi (divided)

dolce (sweet)

dolente (sad)

doloroso (full of grief)

dopo (after)

doppel (double)

doux (sweet)

duro (hard, harsh)

espressivo (with expression)

fermo (firm, decided)

forza (force)

fuoco (fire)

gioco (playful)

giusto (strict, exact)

grandioso (majestically)

grazioso (elegantly)

grosso (grand, full)

gusto (taste)

incalzando (mor vehement)

l'istesso (the same)

lagrimoso (tearful)

lamentoso (mournfully)

legando (legato, connected)

legato (connected)

lunga (long)

ma (but)

maestoso (majestic)

marcato (marked)

meno (less)

molto (very much)

morbido (soft, tender)

mosso (moved)

moto (motion, speed)

non (not)

parlando (speaking)

parlato (spoken)

pesante (heavy)

piacere, a (at pleasure)

piu (more)

poco (little)

quasi (nearly)

riposo (calm)

ritmico (rhythmical)

senza (without)

sotto (below, under)

subito (suddenly)

tanto (too, so much)

tenuto (held)

tornando (returning)

troppo (too)

Terms that do not fit nicely into one particular category

acappella

arpeggio

attacca (attached)

basso continuo

coloratura

counterpoint

drone

liturgy

loco (as written)

mode

pedal tone

penultimate (next to last)

pitch cell

polychord

scale

segue (follows)

tacit (omit)

texture

thematic development

timbre

tone cluster

tonic

tutti (all)

voce (voice)

Chapter 9
ଔ
Bibliographic References

Histories

General History

Abraham, Gerald. *The Concise Oxford History of Music.* Oxford and New York: Oxford University Press, 1985.

Bonds, Mark Evan. *A History of Music in Western Culture.* Upper Saddle River, NJ: Prentice Hall, 2003.

Grout, Donald Jay; and Palisca, Claude V. *A History of Western Music.* 6th ed. New York and London: W. W. Norton, 2001.

Lang, Paul Henry. *Music in Western Civilization.* New York: W. W. Norton, 1941.

Machlis, Joseph; and Forney, Kristine. *The Enjoyment of Music: An Introduction to Perceptive Listening.* 9th ed. New York and London: W. W. Norton, 2003.

Antiquity

Mathiesen, Thomas, J. *Apollo's Lyre: Greek Music and Music Theory in Antiquity and the Early Middle Ages.* Lincoln: University of Nebraska Press, 1999.

Pöhlmann, Egert; and West, Martin L. *Documents of Ancient Greek Music.* Oxford: Clarendon Press, 2001.

Medieval

Apel, Willi. *The Notation of Polyphonic Music 900-1600.* 5th ed. Cambridge: The Mediaeval Academy of America, 1953.

Crocker, Richard; and Hiley, David, eds. *The Early Middle Ages to 1300.* Oxford: Oxford University Press, 1990.

Hoppin, Richard H. *Medieval Music.* New York: W. W. Norton, 1978.

Hughes, Andrew. *Medieval Music: The Sixth Liberal Art.* Toronto: University of Toronto Press, 1980.

Levy, Kenneth. *Gregorian Chant and the Carolingians*. Princeton: Princeton University Press, 1998.

McKinnon, James, ed. *Antiquity and the Middle Ages: From Ancient Greece to the 15th Century*. Englewood Cliffs, NJ: Prentice Hall, 1990.

Renaissance

Apel, Willi. *The Notation of Polyphonic Music 900-1600*. 5th ed. Cambridge: The Mediaeval Academy of America, 1953.

Brown, Howard M.; and Stein, Louise. *Music in the Renaissance*. rev. ed. Upper Saddle River, NJ: Prentice Hall, 1999.

Brown, Howard M. *Instrumental Music Printed before 1600*. Cambridge: Harvard University Press, 1965.

Fenlon, Iain, ed. *Music in Medieval and Early Modern Europe: Patronage, Sources, and Texts*. Cambridge: Cambridge University Press, 1981.

Perkins, Leeman. *Music in the Age of the Renaissance*. New York: W. W. Norton, 1998.

Roche, Jerome. *North Italian Church Music in the Age of Monteverdi*. Oxford: Clarendon Press, 1984.

Strohm, Reinhard. *The Rise of European Music, 1380-1500*. Cambridge: Cambridge University Press, 1993.

Baroque

Anthony, James R. *French Baroque Music from Beaujoyeulx to Rameau*. rev. ed. Portland, OR: Amadeus Press, 1997.

Baron, John. Baroque Music: *A Research and Information Guide*. New York: Garland, 1993.

Bianconi, Lorenzo. *Music in the Seventeenth Century*. Cambridge: Cambridge University Press, 1987.

Blume, Friedrich. *Protestant Church Music*. New York: W. W. Norton, 1974.

Carter, Tim. *Music in Late Renaissance and Early Baroque Italy*. London: Batsford, 1992.

Newman, William S. *The Sonata in the Baroque Era*. 3rd ed. New York: W. W. Norton, 1983.

Palisca, Claude V. *Baroque Music*, 3rd ed. Englewood Cliffs, NJ: Prentice Hall, 1991.

Sadie, Julie Anne. *Companion to Baroque Music*. London: Dent, 1990.

Smither, Howard E. *A History of the Oratorio*, 3 vols. Chapel Hill: University of North Carolina Press, 1977-87.

Sternfeld, Frederick W. *The Birth of Opera.* Oxford: Clarendon Press, 1993.

Tomlinson, Gary. *Monteverdi and the End of the Renaissance.* Berkeley: University of California Press, 1987.

Classic

Allanbrook, Wye Jamison. *Rhythmic Gesture in Mozart: 'Le Nozze de Figaro' and 'Don Giovanni'.* Chicago and London: University of Chicago Press, 1983.

Blume, Friderich. *Classic and Romantic Music.* New York: W. W. Norton, 1970.

Burney, Charles. *General History of Music.* (1776-82). 2 vols. ed. by Frank Mercer. New York: Dover, 1957.

Downs, Philip. *Classical Music: The Era of Haydn, Mozart, and Beethoven.* New York: W. W. Norton, 1992.

Heartz, Daniel. *Haydn, Mozart, and the Viennese School, 1740-1780.* New York: W. W. Norton, 1992.

Pestelli, Giorgio. *The Age of Mozart and Beethoven.* Cambridge: Cambridge University Press, 1984.

Ratner, Leonard G. *Classic Music: Expression, Form, and Style.* New York: Schirmer Books, 1980.

Zaslaw, Neal, ed. *The Classical Era: From the 1740s to the End of the 18th Century.* Englewood Cliffs, NJ: Prentice Hall, 1989.

19th Century/Romantic

Blume, Friderich. *Classic and Romantic Music.* New York: W. W. Norton, 1970.

Dahlhaus, Carl. *Nineteenth-Century Music.* transl. by J. Bradford Robinson. Berkeley: University of California Press, 1989.

Longyear, Rey M. *Nineteenth-Century Romanticism in Music.* 3rd ed. Englewood Cliffs, NJ: Prentice Hall, 1988.

Plantinga, Leon. *Romantic Music: A History of Music Style in Nineteenth-Century Europe.* New York: W. W. Norton, 1984.

Ratner, Leonard G. *Romantic Music: Sound and Syntax.* New York: Schirmer Books, 1992.

Ringer, Alexander, ed. *The Early Romantic Era.* Englewood Cliffs, NJ: Prentice Hall, 1990.

Rosen, Charles. *The Romantic Generation.* Cambridge: Harvard University Press, 1995.

Samson, Jim, ed. The Late Romantic Era. Englewood Cliffs, NJ: Prentice Hall, 1991.

20th Century

Antokoletz, Elliott. *Twentieth-Century Music.* Englewood Cliffs, NJ: Prentice Hall, 1992.

Morgan, Robert P. *Twentieth-Century Music: A History of Music Style in Modern Europe and America.* New York: W. W. Norton, 1991.

Salzman, Eric. *Twentieth-Century: An Introduction.* 4th ed. Upper Saddle River, NJ: Prentice Hall, 2002.

Simms, Bryan. *Music of the 20th Century: Style and Structure.* New York: Schirmer Books, 1986.

Whittall, Arnold. *Music since the First World War.* London: St. Martin's Press, 1995.

World Music

Alves, William. *Music of the Peoples of the World.* Toronto: Thomson Shirmer, 2006.

Broughton, Simon; and Ellingham, Mark. *Rough Guide to World Music Volume One: Africa, Europe & The Middle East.* Rough Guides, 2000.

Broughton, Simon; and Ellingham, Mark. *Rough Guide to World Music Volume Two: Latin and North America, the Caribbean, Asia & the Pacific.* Rough Guides, 2000.

Fletcher, Peter; and Picken, Laurence. *World Musics in Context: A Comprehensive Survey of the World's Major Musical Cultures.* Oxford University Press, 2004.

Miller, Terry E. *World Music: A Global Journey.* Routledge, 2005.

Nettl, Bruno. *Excursions in World Music,* Prentice Hall, 2000.

Nettl, Bruno; Stone, Ruth M.; Porter, James; and Rice, Timothy, eds. *The Garland Encyclopedia of World Music.* 10 volumes. Routledge, 1999. Volume I, *Africa*; Volume II, *South America, Mexico, Central America, and the Caribbean*; Volume III, *The United States and Canada*; Volume IV, *Southeast Asia*; Volume V, *South Asia, The Indian Subcontinent*; Volume VI, *The Middle East*; Volume VII, *East Asia, China, Japan, and Korea*; Volume VIII, Europe; Volume IX, *Australia and the Pacific Islands*; Volume X, *The World's Music, General Perspectives and Reference Tools.*

Nidel, Richard. *World Music: The Basics.* Routledge, 2004.

Titon, Jeff Todd. *Worlds of Music: An Introduction to the Music of the World's Peoples.* Schirmer, 2005.

Jazz History

Appell, Glenn; and Hemphill, David. *American Popular Music: A Multicultural History.* Thomson Schirmer, 2006.

Brown, John Robert. *A Concise History of Jazz.* Mel Bay Publications, 2004.

Campbell, Michael. *The Beat Goes On: Popular Music in America.* Thomson Schirmer, 2006.

Gioia, Ted. *The History of Jazz.* Oxford University Press. 1998.

Kernfeld, Barry, ed. *The New Grove Dictionary of Jazz*, 2nd ed. New York: Grove's Dictionaries Inc., 2002.

Kirchner, Bill. *The Oxford Companion to Jazz.* Oxford University Press, 2005.

Megill, Donald D.; and Demory, Richard S. *Introduction to Jazz History.* Prentice Hall, 2003.

Schuller, Gunther. *Early Jazz: Its roots and Musical Development.* Oxford University Press, 2005.

Yurochko, Bob. *A Short History of Jazz.* Rowman & Littlefield, 1993.

Reference

General

Duckles, Vincent H.; and Reed, Ira. *Music Reference and Research Materials: An Annotated Bibliography*. 5th ed. New York: Schirmer Books, 1997.

Randel, Don Michael, ed. *The New Harvard Dictionary of Music.* Cambridge and London: The Belknap Press of Harvard University Press, 1986.

Music Theory

Damschroder, David; and Williams, David Russell. *Music Theory from Zarlino to Schenker.* Stuyvesant, NY: Pendragon Press, 1990.

Composers

Sadie, Stanley, ed. *The New Grove Dictionary of Music and Musicians*, 2nd ed. New York and London: W. W. Norton, 2001.

Slonimsky, Nicolas. *Baker's Biographical Dictionary of Musicians*. New York: Schirmer Books, 2001.

Women Composers in Particular

Jezic, Diane Peacock. *Women Composers, the Lost Tradition Found*. New York: The Feminist Press, 1988.

Sadie, Julie, ed; and Samuel, Rhian, ed. *The Norton/Grove Dictionary of Women Composers*. London: The Macmillan Press Limited, 1995.

Instruments

Sadie, Stanley, ed. *The New Grove Dictionary of Musical Instruments*. London: Macmillan Press, 1984.

Alphabetical List of Names with Dates

This is a list of the personalities in alphabetical order. The page numbers indicate where the person is listed in the book.

Index of Terms

Abbreviations

I	tonic
instr.	instrumental
m	minor
M	major
NG	*The New Grove Dictionary of Music and Musicians*, ed. Stanley Sadie, W. W. Norton, 2001.
rit.	ritornello
V	dominant